Standing in a River of Time

POEMS

T0160293

Jónína Kirton

with a foreword by Wanda John-Kehewin

TALONBOOKS

Talonbooks
9259 Shaughnessy Street, Vancouver, British Columbia, Canada V6P 6R4
talonbooks.com

Talonbooks is located on xʷməθkʷəy̓əm, Sḵwx̱wú7mesh, and
səl̓ilwətaʔɬ Lands.

First printing: 2022

Typeset in Arno
Printed and bound in Canada on 100% post-consumer recycled paper

Interior and cover design by Typesmith
Cover illustration by Jan Castillo

Talonbooks acknowledges the financial support of the Canada Council
for the Arts, the Government of Canada through the Canada Book
Fund, and the Province of British Columbia through the British
Columbia Arts Council and the Book Publishing Tax Credit.

LIBRARY AND ARCHIVES CANADA CATALOGUING IN PUBLICATION

Title: Standing in a river of time : poems / Jónína Kirton ; with a
preface by Wanda John-Kehewin.
Names: Kirton, Jónína, 1955- author. | John-Kehewin, Wanda, 1971-
writer of preface.
Identifiers: Canadiana 20210306815 | ISBN 9781772013795 (softcover)
Classification: LCC PS8621.I785 S73 2022 | DDC C811/.6—dc23

STANDING IN A RIVER OF TIME

Also by JÓNÍNA KIRTON

An Honest Woman
page as bone – ink as blood

Published by Talonbooks

This book is dedicated to my husband, Garry Ward.

ALL MY RELATIONS

Please do take care of yourself while reading this book: within it are moments of deep despair, the results of traumatic events. I have intentionally kept the details sparse and only touched on a few pivotal moments. Even so, it may be triggering for some. If you are drawn to this narrative, perhaps our Ancestors have conspired to bring us together. Perhaps you are the one who will bring healing to your family. Perhaps you are already doing this and just needed the reminder that you are not alone; no matter how it looks, there are those who walk with you.

The more I write out of my life, the more I encounter the impossibility of telling the truth. The lived story is far more complex than the fabricated one. This is the seduction of fiction: its containability. The certainty of words black and white on the page. The comfort of no one else's version calling ours into question. That sad yet sweet satisfaction when "The End" used to appear on the last page. I had assumed autobiography to be an inscribing of identity. Suspected it to be an amplification of ego. It is quite the opposite. With every word I write I am reminded of deficiency. Incompleteness. Every word I select is at the expense of others.

—BETSY WARLAND

Bloodroot: Tracing the Untelling of Motherloss (2000)

Foreword

BY WANDA JOHN-KEHEWIN

All our lives, are we human testaments to survival in our never-ending search for love, when we should have searched for it within ourselves? This continuous internal struggle to be at peace is made apparent through the eyes and pen of Jónína Kirton, who gave us bits and pieces of her life in her previous two books of poetry, *page as bone – ink as blood*, and *An Honest Woman*. She now gives us her entire truth in this compilation of the events that brought her to her knees many, many times in her search to give a name to her pain. Her resilience and her willingness to see her truth, flaws and all, will uplift her readers, because she makes it possible for us just to be human. Kirton reminds us that storytelling is alive and well and that it pushes us forward into new territory so we can all stand in our truth, as she does so eloquently and invitingly. She reminds us that for some love isn't readily available, that those who do not even have a sliver of an idea about love are left struggling to define themselves in a world not kind to the "different." Loss and love run through this work, which is about acceptance and healing through truth: "rather let [it] run through you like a river picking up sticks and stones." Through poetry, Kirton teaches others that it is okay not to feel okay; she shows us a way to look at the world and ourselves without judging either. Taking us on a journey of injustices, confusion, and truth, she shows us the way to understand and come to terms with the pains of the past and "heal seven generations" back by being the voice for the voiceless. Kirton gives us the understanding and the words to describe the past in a gentle, loving way – loving even to those who caused her pain.

If a picture paints a thousand words, then Jónína Kirton's poetry creates a thousand pictures with her beautiful choice of words and fresh metaphors that ripple immediate understanding of experiences needing words to heal. From beginning to end, Jónína takes us through the stages of grief and lets the "blood" spill on the page in the gentlest way possible. In *Standing in a River of Time*, Jónína Kirton takes us on a healing journey of sorrow, acceptance, understanding, love, loss, and forgiveness: "Mornings began to speak to me of a new beginning. A fresh start."

Two Women Drowning:
One Survives

We were treading water with no shoreline in sight.

—BETSY WARLAND

Bloodroot (2000)

My mother's cancer has returned. She's called me home to Winnipeg, not to tell me herself, but to send me to her doctor so that he can tell me the news.

Cancer has travelled to her lungs and her liver. She will not agree to any extraordinary measures, no radiation or chemo.

There will be no surgery this time.

When he says, "There is no coming back from this," I feel as if I am falling into darkness. His words, his face, fade as I make my way to the bottom of a deep well. I don't know what I had been expecting, but it wasn't this.

I cannot assimilate all that I'm hearing. I want to scream but cannot open my mouth. I ask no questions.

I have never been able to save her from my father's fists, and now this.

~

I don't recall leaving the doctor's office or the walk to the Polo Park bus loop, but once there, I find I cannot get on the bus. The word "terminal" has become an efficient virus making its way into every nook and cranny of my mind and body.

~

I don't know how long I have been sitting on this bench, the one just outside the A&W drive-in on Portage Avenue. It is the same bench I sat on daily for years as I made my way to work at the Royal Bank downtown. I am in my hometown, at my bus stop, but nothing seems familiar.

Everything has changed.

Why did no one warn me? Where is my father? How could either of them let me go to hear news like this on my own?

I know my mother. She is a nurse. Not only does she have her own radical mastectomy in her mind, but she has also been at the bedside of many terminal patients. She knows what *no extraordinary measures* means. I do not; I will soon learn.

It's 1985, a time before cellphones, and there is no way to call or text anyone. I decide to go to the mall to look for a pay phone.

I need to talk to someone.

The mall is awash with happy shoppers. Some are within arm's reach, but none would know to catch me should I fall.

My closest friend Laurie always knows what to do. I find a pay phone, but she doesn't answer, and I don't leave a message. That would be unfair.

I head to the washroom to wash my now-puffy face. I stare into the mirror, attempt to talk myself into going home.

I know my mother is there waiting for me.

She has already lost two sons in their teens and survived breast cancer. She will be worried. I have to go home. I whisper to myself, "You can do this! You can ..."

On the bus ride home we pass the Assiniboine Park Zoo where I once saw a buffalo calf being born. The park and Charleswood hold so many memories for me. I try to hang on to the happier memories as I walk up Haney Street believing I can be strong, that I can be what my mother needs. But the second I see her face, I know that this is too much.

I rush past her

      run up the stairs

to the bathroom.

My body is rejecting the news.

My mother sits on the edge of the bathtub rubbing my back. It should be me comforting her, but all I can do is throw up and cry. We sit together, two women in a family with four men, two already dead. Once again, we are bonding over grief. Once again, my tears and her tears are merging. Two women alone, together in a family of men.

My baby brother is probably at the golf course or the hockey rink, and Dad is no doubt at the pub. He will be home after the bar closes and may have friends with him. There will be laughter in our living room just as there was the night of Murray's funeral. My mother will once again be in the kitchen crying while my father drinks with his friends. That is the best-case scenario.

If he comes home alone, he will be angry.

⌒

I return to Edmonton, to my job at the bank, and to finish wedding plans. I am thirty-one and about to marry again. My soon-to-be second husband has advised me that he intends to keep his yearly vacation schedule: six weeks in Hawai'i – I am welcome to join him for two of the weeks. He will also need a week in whatever city hosts the Grey Cup, and to attend the Indianapolis 500, an event that he has attended every year, sometimes as a mechanic in the pit.

I am not invited.

These are "guys only" events that he needs after working hard to earn the money for this "much-needed" time off. I still don't understand why I agreed to these terms.

⌒

The wedding is his first, my second. He is an Italian Catholic, and I am a lapsed Anglican. It will be a huge traditional wedding, something I said I would never do, but for him I am letting go of many things.

Over and over, I am told how lucky I am that this man wants to marry me. All the Italian mothers and grandmothers who come to the two-hundred-person wedding shower tell me that he is a catch and that they *had* to meet the woman who finally landed their "Italian Stallion."

My mother is thin; her small hand holds mine as we sit within this world we do not know. There is so much gold, the gifts more like wedding gifts. We are not accustomed to this. I think my mother is ashamed that she cannot buy something more extravagant. My father has a good job, as an air traffic controller at the Winnipeg Airport, but he drinks.

The night before my wedding, Aunt Myrna gives me a book she has come across in her work as a psychologist. Written for "Adult Children of Alcoholics," *The Struggle for Intimacy* outlines the deficits we have as survivors of an alcoholic parent. The book keeps me up all night. Key phrases jump out at me:

→ "I love you. Go away." I see why I have become the mixed-message queen;
→ Some people "never got to be a child" and have "an edge of sadness to them";
→ It gets worse: "Adult children guess at what normal is."

There is more. We have a high need for control and overreact to changes we have no control over. We are people pleasers, impulsive, but at least we are "loving and loyal."

None of it is reassuring. We are loyal even when we shouldn't be. Even our loyalty is suspect.

I can see that I have no business getting married. I am too broken. But it is too late, everyone is here from out of town. More importantly, my mother is happy that her daughter has found a good man and is finally settling down. I want to make my mother happy, to bring her peace.

Our wedding photos are revealing. Dad is hungover. His face is puffy. I have too much makeup on. Mom is thin and frail.

They both walk me down the aisle towards the altar. Mel looks like a smoky-eyed movie star in that tuxedo. His body open, his face lit up, he greets me, takes my hand. I relax, think, "He loves me, maybe everything will be okay."

That night I drink too much. I do not remember leaving this wedding, just as I do not remember leaving my first wedding at age eighteen. For some reason, both husbands liked me to drink. Apparently, I am the life of the party. What no one knows is that inside I am always afraid, that fear has its tentacles in everything I say and do. I am like my father, a liar. All good drunks are liars.

Months later my mother calls me home again. She has written her obituary and is leaving AA pamphlets in her dresser drawer. Ever the optimist, she hopes my dad will find them and read them. Her years in Al-Anon taught her how to be a good wife to the alcoholic. She wants me to know that she loves him. I am taken aback by this assertion but remain quiet. This is her moment. She has things she wants to say. I am here to listen.

She has instructions for everything. She explains that she intends to stay home as long as she can. When she enters the hospital in her final days, I am to sit by her bed. I am not to leave her alone, as she has seen happen with so many of the seniors she cared for at Tuxedo Villa. She does not want to die alone and knows that my eighteen-year-old brother and my alcoholic father cannot be trusted to be there.

There is more. She wants to know if I am happy. Do I think I drink too much? How is my marriage? Are things okay?

I lie. Say that I am okay, that I don't drink too much. I still believe I am not like my father. As for my marriage, well, it is not what I expected, but I reassure her. She has other things to worry about.

We sit at the kitchen table, two women alone in a family dominated by the needs of men. We both know our love for one another is deep and enduring but it will soon be tested. We have never been here before. We have no maps for this new territory of grief we are about to share. I will be returning to my job at the bank in Edmonton and she will be here, at the kitchen table, waiting for my father to come home, hoping he is not angry, not going to hit her. I will keep my job, and my marriage to this man whose need for control is becoming clearer each day. We will wait for her death. As I say goodbye, I do not know that I will never hear her voice in person again.

There are daily phone calls. Some days she speaks of how grateful she is for the care my father is showing her, and then … there are the days she tells me that, as thin and frail as she is, he still pushes her around. There is nothing that I can do with this information; there never has been anything I can do. She loves him.

A few months later, I get the call I have been dreading. Mom has been admitted to Grace Hospital and doesn't have long. I pack a bag, head to the Edmonton Airport, alone. I have already left my husband and entered therapy and am attending Adult Children of Alcoholics, where I have a male sponsor who is very kind to me. I do not need anywhere to stay in Winnipeg because I will do as she asked and sleep beside her bed in a cot.

That night and every day before her passing, I pray for some last words, to hear her say she loves me just one more time. I long for her to put her cheek on my cheek the way she often did.

People come and go. I am, most times, the ghost in the room, waiting with the dead.

I do not know if I can live without her.

My grandpa Cecil and I sit in the hospital café while I take a short break to eat. He is smiling, which is not usual for him. I find this especially odd as he is about to lose his favourite daughter, Dolly, as he loved to call my mom.

Something is different.

We all love him but are afraid of him. He was always a rough man with a glass eye, hardened fingers from farm work, and hugs that hurt. He held everyone too tight. To a child this was terrifying. He is softer now. I am curious. I ask what has changed in his life. He tells me that one day he woke up and as he rubbed the sleep from his eyes it hit him, "I could just choose to be happy, to remember that life is a gift."

I learn many years later that he had suffered from depression. He was hospitalized and had received electric shock treatments.

His oldest son, my uncle Hugh, says, "There was always a sadness at home." My aunt Myrna spoke of his rage. Life as a dirt-poor farmer during the Depression was more than he could handle. His children, including my mother, had suffered at his hands. No one knew that he, too, was suffering.

⁓

My mom has many brothers and sisters. The oldest living child of seventeen siblings, she is the most loved of them all.

Many come to say goodbye.

⁓

Late at night it is just me and Mom. Most nights I can't sleep, so I just watch her breathe, fearing each one could be the last. If I do fall asleep, I awaken with a startle and the first thing I do is check to see if her chest is still rising and falling. As she gets closer to death, her breathing becomes harder to witness; the rising, the falling grows increasingly subtle. Sometimes I have to touch her to be sure she is still alive.

The doctor says she can hear us, so we should be careful what we say. Even so, I say things I later regret. I beg. I plead with her not to leave me. I pray, and as I pray something begins to shift.

Mornings began to speak to me of a new beginning. A fresh start.

⁓

Time has become meaningless. Gratitude is growing and everything around me is talking to me. The hum of the traffic on Portage Avenue has become a vibrational hymn. When I take a shower, the gentle touch of the water takes some of my pain away.

Subtle shifts are taking place within my body, my spirit, as I contemplate life without my mother. So much of my life has centred on her pain. Who will I be without her?

⁓

One night I tell my sober uncle that I am afraid that my drinking has crossed the line. I do this in the room with my mother, forgetting that in her deep sleep she can hear every word. But my father never forgets to say and do the right things. Every day he comes by for a little while.

When he arrives, he stands in the doorway and takes a deep breath before entering, boisterous. "Good morning, Lorraine! You look beautiful!" We know when he is coming, so put makeup on her ashen face. We know that looking good is important to her; it is to all the Denham women.

Our attempts look foolish. She looks like the doll I had when I was little. How I loved that doll even though she was missing most of her hair. I had put makeup on her, too. I used red nail polish to make her lips red and crayons for eyeshadow and a little too much blush. She looked awful, but I loved her. We never had many toys. She was my only doll. I only have one Mom. What will I do without her?

<hr/>

Time passes slowly at night, and I have bronchitis. I always get bronchitis when I go to Winnipeg. Louise Hay says that wherever we have weakness in the body, it can tell us something.

Lungs are about Father.

I cough all night one night and am half asleep when a kind nurse's hand touches mine. It is dark and I cannot see her, but she hands me some cough candies. Such a small thing, but it makes me cry. Someone is caring for me.

That morning my father spits words at me. He asks, "What do you think you are doing staying here every night? What are you trying to prove?" I have no answers for him. I guess my mom never told him what she wanted. I go drinking that night.

<hr/>

The doctor is called to her room. Everyone is sombre. The nurses will not look me in the eye as the doctor pulls the covers from my mother's feet as if he is a mechanic looking under the hood of a car. Her feet are black. He announces, "It won't be long now."

I am ready to let her go. I have made peace with the fact that there is no coming back from this. There is no more to say. She will not tell me she loves me ever again. I will not hear her speak or see her smile. All that is left to do is sit by her bed.

I have no idea what is coming next or how her final moments will change me forever.

My memories are vague. It has been ten long days and sleepless nights. By now I am numb, but even so, I can feel the energy in the room shift as an uncommon peace enters the room. Something or someone is welcoming my mother home. I feel her beingness float out of her body. She hovers there for a moment before heading towards the ceiling. Her spirit merging with whoever has come for her. Together they fill the room with a comforting warmth.

I believe she is gone when I am suddenly startled by a final gasp. I did not know this was coming and am confused for a moment but soon realize her body is empty. She is not there.

She is no longer in the room.

I have just witnessed something otherworldly. I now know that we are not our body. We are so much more. I desperately want to know what is next. Where is she?

While making arrangements for her funeral at the St. Mary Anglican Church, I ask her minister if he has any insight into what I experienced in her final moments. He was a "man of God" and I knew he and my mother had been close. She once told me that, in private, he called her his "Passion Flower," a flower linked to the ten faithful Apostles.

He must know something.

As I share with her minister how peace had filled the room just as she was leaving her body, he grows restless, will not make any eye contact. I find myself wondering how much he knew about our lives. Soon it is clear that he has no answers for me and is not equipped to offer support. He, too, is grieving.

We move on to discuss what could be done to commemorate her. We already have plaques at the church for my brothers, Gordon and Murray, who had been altar boys there. Now half of our family of six will be there on plaques that will eventually mean nothing to those who attend this church. At thirty-two I was all too aware that time passes and that we will all be forgotten one day. I already knew that people come to funeral services, hearts full of sadness for your loss, but soon their lives go on, unchanged, while yours is never the same.

You cannot return to what is no longer there.

⁓

At her service there is a receiving line. I stand next to my brother Robert, who stands next to my father. Robert is just eighteen and has already lost two brothers and his mother. At ten years old, he once asked me if bad luck comes in threes. This asked after having lost two brothers. I could see the question that was weighing on his tiny, ten-year-old self.

Was he next?

Maybe he was right and Mom was the third. Maybe the rest of us will live long.

As people stop by to shake hands, offer hugs and condolences, my father introduces my brother and ignores me. Seeing this, my brother takes on the task of introducing me.

My father's eyes are cold when he looks at me. It hurts, but I say nothing. I try to be my mother's daughter, the one she taught how to behave at church teas. She would want that.

Later at dinner my uncle John is angry with my father. He says, "She just lost her mother. Why are you treating her this way?"

Now I am afraid.

I know my father will blame me for this embarrassing moment. I have no memory of what follows. When things get tense, I not only turn ashen, I black out. I am missing many moments in my life.

⁓

The night of the service, I go to the nightclub with my friends. My baby brother goes to the bar with his, and my father heads to the Charleswood Hotel to drink and watch the strippers. This is how we Kirtons handle grief. We don't.

SEEKERS

these people
swimming
all six of them
until one drowns
threatens to pull
the others down

in the riptide of loss
there were no instructions
in the holy book
none that pertain
to the mixing of blood

yet Mother insisted
we go to church where
she placed a plaque
for Gordon
the altar boy
the river took

she kept praying
as we all headed for the rapids
caught in the turbulence
of Father's rage

Murray decided to head for the shore
just eighteen he drove his truck
across the country to join the PNE
once there he noticed
he did not fit
he did not feel safe

his calls to me   his big sister
frantic   fear had him
soon he was seeking safety
at our uncle's ranch where
he did not drown but was shot
leaving an unfillable hole

his return home in a box
greeted at the airport by my father
Mother's tears flooding
all the rooms of our home
                now we were all drowning

IN THE FORGETTING PLACE

what am I without you?
who will I be when you are gone?

will my bones tell our story?
will it be true?
will I recognize it?

in the forgetting place
there is no light
no one listening

what am I without you?
who will I be when you are gone?

ASHES IN MY MOUTH

your death ash in my mouth
until I look up and a cooling cascade
of water begins to wash you away .
but I am not ready to let you go
so quickly close my mouth
trapping what is left of the ash
now made muddy by sky tears

I am afraid to spit you out
welcome the feel of grit on my teeth
defend my need for you
not interested in letting go I sink
into the feelings most avoid
many ask why
I have no answers until
forty years later I see
what their attempts
to wash away losses have left behind

it does not work
some things resist revision

if it hurts   it hurts   until it doesn't

The Power of Prayer:
Self-Effort and Grace

Just as a bird soars on two wings, a seeker is liberated through self-effort and grace.

—GURUMAYI CHIDVILASANANDA

Self-Effort & Grace: Two Wings of the Bird (1992)

I used to tell people that my mother went straight to heaven and, being the good Christian woman that she was, she had God's ear. I still have a Technicolor burning-bush image of her, surrounded by light, tapping God on the shoulder with one hand and with the other hand pointing to Earth. "See that one there. That one is my daughter, and she *really* needs your help." Why else would I find myself in a bar, a week after she passed away, talking to a newly minted member of Narcotics Anonymous?

I have had a lot to drink when I meet the man who will take me to my first Narcotics Anonymous (NA) meeting. Slipping, sliding off my stool, my body made liquid after numerous drinks, I have the audacity to proudly tell him I know about the Twelve Steps. Slurring my words, I say, "My dad is an alcoholic" and that "I have been going to ACOA." As soon as the words leave my mouth, I know that he knows I am a liar. All good drunks are liars. We know one another when we meet. I am not surprised when he asks for my phone number.

When my roommate and I get home, I tell her he asked for my number. She laughs. "I knew he liked you. He wants to ask you out." Even though he never said it, I knew he wanted to take me to a meeting. His eyes told me everything I needed to know. In the end we were both right. He did want to date me, but he also wanted to help me get sober.

My first meeting felt like a scene from *28 Days*, only I was not Sandra Bullock and this was not a movie. In 1987, NA was still fairly new to Edmonton. There were only a few of us, a core group of about ten men and women, who attended the same meetings and hung out together. Until recently, whatever their addiction, everyone had simply gone to AA. But like always, some purist started to ban certain "outside issues," and the mention of drugs or ACOA was discouraged.

But I digress. There I was at my first meeting with "drug addicts," the people my dad had taught me to fear. He had witnessed drug addiction in the navy and often warned me against using drugs. I am grateful for the teachings he gave me.

———

Despite knowing better, I did once shoot speed. It was after my second brother had died and I was at a party with my biker boyfriend, an ex–speed freak. His friend, an old long-haired hippy drug dealer, convinced me to try a hit. We shared a needle. It was the mid-seventies and none of us knew anything about the dangers of sharing needles.

I can still see that smoky room, the beads in the doorways and the faint images of others, many of whom were slumped over. Alcohol had always been my drug of choice, but that night I gave in to peer pressure. The high was instantaneous. My body awash in what felt like warm, liquid light. I was free of all my pain. To this day I have never felt anything close to the bliss I experienced, but given what my dad had shared with me I knew it would be best if I never did it again. Not only that, poor Steve, my biker boyfriend, told me later that he had spent the night in the bathroom, where he rocked himself as he shook uncontrollably. The temptation to relapse had been unbearable for him. We never went to a party like that again.

———

My first sponsor was a strict task master and well versed in the AA Twelve Steps. Within in a few months, she had me doing my Step Four, an inventory of my life. There are many ways to do a Step Four. Over the years I have done a number of them, but it is that first one that I remember the most.

It was all new to me. I had never looked at my life as a whole. I had been taught to just keep moving, which meant I knew nothing about reflection and the gift of seeing patterns, attending to grief and resentments. But I was desperate and willing to try just about anything.

With this Step Four I did not use any templates, I simply wrote down all the losses, the things that I had done to others, and the things that had been done to me. No wonder I felt cursed. A lot had happened, but the enormity of it all didn't sink in until I did my Step Five.

The Alcoholics Anonymous Big Book's instructions for Step Five say that we are to admit "to God, to ourselves, and to another human being the exact nature of our wrongs." I and others sometimes struggle with the old language and the Christian tone of the teachings in the Big Book. Many soften the language and suggest those doing a Five not only admit to their wrongs but also that they include everything that they are ashamed of or that has caused them pain.

My first Step Five took two full days. I had a lot to share.

My dear sponsor sat with me on my couch and listened. She listened and listened for hours. Sometimes she cried and when she cried, I would not stop talking. I didn't cry. I just kept going, thinking, "Why? Why is she crying?"

Her tears and my confusion were a gift that silently seeped into my consciousness.

"Why? Why is she crying?" – the kind of question you don't ask out loud but rather let run through you like a river picking up sticks and stones.

Her tears and my confusion opened a doorway to an experience that has carried me to this day.

Once we were finished, as is customary, we prayed together and then she left. Now alone in my eighth-floor apartment, I contemplated her tears and was struck by the enormity of the pain I carried in my tiny body. Five-foot-two and just over a hundred pounds, I was not only numb, but I was running out of room for new pain and needed to deal with this old pain. But how? The thought of facing it all made me want to drink.

I headed to the kitchen, opened the fridge hoping to see that bottle of wine my roommate usually had on standby. It was there, lying on the bottom shelf, acting so innocent while wafting promises of oblivion. Yes, I was that kind of drinker. A blackout drinker who sought to erase herself.

It was tempting to go back.

I hung onto the fridge door for quite a while, contemplating whether or not to bend down and pick up the bottle. I never touched it. I decided instead to lie on my bed in a fetal position.

They say AA ruins your drinking, and it does. It was too late. I couldn't go back. I knew too much. I had to pray.

Prayer is most powerful when charged with emotion, and I was deep in fear with nowhere to go. That was until a white light presented itself. To this day I don't know if the white light originated in my heart or entered my heart, but whatever the case, it brought peace. Not the drug-induced bliss of speed but rather a softer, even more gentle feeling of being held. It felt familiar.

In those days I believed in a Christian God and would pray on my knees resting my head on my arms on the bed which I imagined to be God's lap. I thought that I needed a father who loved me, one who could guide me. The white light had no gender. It just was. I was beginning to see that I was well supported by something I need not define. Thank Goddess AA supports us in finding our own "higher power."

⌒

In recovery, I learned to lean into prayer. I was told to pray daily and to ask God for help. I not only prayed to God; I also talked to my mother. I began to understand that just as she could hear me while she was unconscious, she could hear me now.

I told her everything, just as I always had before I began drinking too much and hiding my pain from her. I asked for her help and for her forgiveness.

I once asked to know her pain. My request came from a sincere desire to see things as they were. I was tired of the glossing over, the diminishing of pain, that my family regularly practised. Within seconds I was on my knees in the kitchen. A lightning bolt had shot through my entire body, leaving me unable to stand. She had endured so much. There was so much to heal. Somehow, I knew that she would be my best guide as I began to heal from the intergenerational trauma that we shared.

What I did not know was how long it would all take. All I knew was that I wanted to free her and myself of pain. I later learned about the Indigenous teaching that says when we heal, we heal seven generations forward and seven back. I take comfort in these teachings.

SLIDING TOWARDS THE END

pushed towards empty I lean
just as I used to on the back of your motorcycle
you and I reckless in the pursuit of one another
that rainy day rush hour traffic on Portage Avenue
one of us leaned too far   dumped the bike

       I slid between cars

prayed to stay in my lane

later a strip of white on my denim coat
evidence of a fall that nearly ended it all

IN SEARCH OF PRAISE

So long as you are praised think only that you are
not yet on your own path but on that of another.

—FRIEDRICH NIETZSCHE

Human, All Too Human: A Book for Free Spirits (1878)

hands clasped I pray for goodness
until my mind wanders to the "to do" list
an internal document of my sins
the forgotten promises   mainly to myself
I was going to exercise every day
read all those self-help books
attend more meetings
where slogans on walls
offer a path towards serenity

hands clasped I pray
to be more myself
less what you want me to be

LOST

deeds cannot dream what dreams can do

—E.E. CUMMINGS

"as freedom is a breakfast food," *Selected Poems* (1994)

within this body many stories
some true   some not
but they all matter

     why some hide

I wish I knew   (maybe I don't)

not knowing what to wish for I avoid it all
make busy with deadlines meant to motivate

stopping now   dropping into now
I feel the inner nudges asking for a new way
reminding me that dreams can motivate

time can unfurl   it doesn't need my help
it passes   tick-tocking
while I making busy don't stop to cry
while I making busy forget to dream

     until forgetting becomes all that I am

GRACE

pure potential exists in the light
whispers   listen to the wind
enter the great river of change
find the centre   float

TIMELESS

Be still, they say.

—LINDA HOGAN

*Dwellings: A Spiritual History of
the Living World* (2007)

timeless

restless

the women of my lineage wait
their histories not recorded
erased on paper they live on in my body
lovers of the sacred they hold me

be still they say

for only in the stillness can you hear
and we have much to say

FOR THE ANCESTORS

transported by your love
transmuted by your grace
I can endure more   much more
perhaps with your love I could even soar
the burned tips of my wings healed
perhaps I could fly, stay above it all
perhaps there I will see more
perhaps you will find me beautiful
something for your eyes to follow
perhaps my voice will grow strong in the sky
and you will hear my unique way with words
perhaps you will see me ˙ hear me
perhaps you will say   all is well

       she did well

Displaced: It's Always about the Land

The Métis were not Indian enough to be acknowledged as having land rights, and they were too Indian to benefit from any policy other than slum clearance. One thing was certain: they were not wanted in the city.

—JEAN TEILLET

The North-West Is Our Mother: The Story of Louis Riel's People, the Métis Nation (2019)

As the oldest child, I was a witness to my parents' marriage and their unified pursuit of an upwardly mobile life. They had both grown up poor, and the promises of a picture-book life in suburbia had a hold on them. My mother poured over fashion magazines and took interior decorating courses in preparation for the life we were going to have in Winnipeg, the birthplace and heart of the Métis Nation.

I was fourteen when we had saved enough for a down payment for that longed-for home, a home that was only possible because, as a Korean War vet, Dad was entitled to a quarter acre of land. Like many Métis, joining the military had been his best option as a young man. Once out of the navy, he struggled with PTSD, having witnessed what he described as violence against civilians. Civilians who looked like him.

After the military, he had a hard time finding and keeping jobs. Mom was at times the sole income earner. This hurt him. He wanted to be the provider for his family. In those days, having a wife at home in suburbia meant you had made it. He was ambitious and never gave up, which meant we were always moving; there was always a new job, a better job.

In Portage la Prairie, Land of the Očhéthi Šakówiŋ, Anishinaabeg ᐊᓂᔑᓈᐯᒃ, and Métis, Dad had done construction work with my uncle Claude, a hard-drinking Québécois man married to Grandma Rose's sister, Aunt Eva. When I was a toddler, we also spent some time in Kuugjuaq ᑯᒡᔪᐊᖅ (Churchill, Manitoba), where Dad was a fireman. Sometimes Dad went alone to work in places like Iqaluit (known then as Frobisher Bay) Δˤb⊃Δᶜ, Nunavut, on the Land of the Inuit. Always a heavy drinker, he worried my mom. Once, on the drive home from Churchill, he crashed his car and came home with cuts all over his face. I didn't understand it all. Her tears, his face – swollen and bruised, covered in stitches. It scared me.

Truth is, I never felt safe in my own home. Dad was volatile, unpredictable. Mom was a good fifties wife, so what Dad wanted was gospel. This got worse when he truly was the "man of the house" and got that good job as an air traffic controller.

Fort William (now part of Thunder Bay, Ontario), on the Land of the Anishinaabeg ◁σᔑᒑⓋᵇ and Métis, was where he took his training in air traffic control. His time in the navy with radar proved to be the ticket to a good job. Once done his training, his first posting was at CFB Goose Bay in Labrador, on the Land of the Innu and NunatuKavummiut. It was there that we spent many years saving for our down payment so that when he could get that transfer to the Winnipeg Airport, we could buy a home.

I wept when, at thirteen, I had to leave Goose Bay.

⌒

Every move brought loss. The first move fractured my sense of self. I believe I was around five or six when we left Portage la Prairie for good. I was leaving behind my homeland, the place where I had been held close by my Métis family, which included aunts, uncles, cousins, my grandma Rose and step-grandfather Fred the fireman, and a Métis, Michif-speaking, fiddle-playing great-grandfather, Elie Godin. It would only be many years later, while reclaiming my Métis ancestry, that I would understand what I had lost.

I am pretty sure we moved to the army base in Thunder Bay, but it might have been social housing. Whatever it was, it was not what I was used to. I was lonely. No longer could I just walk down the street to those welcoming homes filled with the kind of love that helps you stay whole. In this new town, I felt afraid a lot and had to defend my little brother, Gordon, not only from his schoolmates, but also from our father. Something about Gordon irritated Dad. He was not manly enough. He preferred to hang out with the women in the kitchen. So many times, I witnessed Dad yank Gordon out of his chair in the kitchen and drag him out the front door. He would then lock the door and leave Gordon standing outside, by himself, looking forlorn. Gordon was such a sweet kid, always joking around, giggling his way through life. I did my best to protect him.

When I was older and Mom told me Dad hated being *Native*, I wondered if Gordon's dark skin was what set him off. He was very brown, and I think he may have had a learning disability. All I know is that he could not learn how to tell time and failed kindergarten. This embarrassed our dad, and we all knew that when embarrassed, Dad would get mean, real mean.

Every time we moved, I had to make new friends. This was not easy for me, as I was a shy child and the awareness of our unacceptability as *Indians* grew with each move. But we all had to sacrifice if we were ever going to be homeowners.

I had no idea that the pursuit of land was behind so much dysfunction in our society. I also did not know that my family had had many land scrips granted to them a few generations back or that we were moving back to our homeland.

———

Dad finally got that transfer to Winnipeg in 1967. Once there, we rented a townhouse on Portage Avenue. It was to be temporary, just somewhere to live until they bought a house. I was twelve and had already changed schools so many times. Now a pimply faced pre-teen with thick glasses, I had trouble making friends but I always had my brothers. Moving so much and having to keep our home life secret was a bond that only those who grow up in such homes could ever understand.

———

My parents agreed on most things except where to live. Where to build this longed-for home was fraught with difference.

My dad would say, "I don't want my kids living on the wrong side of the tracks" like he had. My mom, a prairie farm girl, was more frugal and wanted to live in cheaper parts of town. They argued. He won.

Eventually, they found a treed lot in Charleswood very near to the edge of town – so close that when the house was built and we had moved in, Dad bought us a snowmobile. No one was allowed to drive snowmobiles in town, but we could easily sneak half a block, hidden in the deep ditch, until we got to the big field where we would race with other snowmobilers.

Sometimes we engaged in death-defying tricks on our snowmobile. Perhaps that is where I began my love affair with the exhilaration danger can bring. There were always arguments: "No, it's my turn to drive," or "It's my turn to sit in the caboose." Once going fast enough, we would pull the plug, releasing the caboose. Sometimes the caboose passed the snowmobile, all occupants waving and laughing, totally unaware of how dangerous this was.

We did not have helicopter parents. We were free to roam and do all we pleased as long as no one reported us and we were home for dinner on time.

~

My parents seemed to always have so many decisions to make and all the important discussions took place at the kitchen table. Children were not included, but I was nosy, so I would sometimes hang around the corner, out of sight, listening. Something about being the oldest child made me feel entitled to know more than my brothers. This was a feeling that was reinforced by Mother confiding in me when she needed a friend.

Once we purchased the lot in Charleswood, we would all pile into the car to go *look at our land*. There were no seat belts – two adults in the front seats and us kids in the back seat, punching each other or hanging out windows. Those back seats were spacious, and with four of us we needed the space. A toddler (Robert), a thirteen-year-old (me), an eleven-year-old (Gordon), and a nine-year-old (Murray). None of us wanted to be doing this, but as the oldest child and the temperature-taker of my parents' relationship, I knew these visits to *our land* brought them together. I knew being landowners, homeowners, was important to them both. I had been listening to them talk about it most of my life.

The contractor wanted to clear-cut our treed lot, but my father did not like this idea. He spent a month, in the hot sun, cutting down only the necessary trees. Apparently he may have been following some genetic imperative – I recently learned from Ariel Gordon, author of *Treed: Walking in Canada's Urban Forests*, that my great-great-aunt, Mary Ann Kirton Good (1841–1932), with the assistance of my great-great-grandfather, Peter Kirton (1839–1925), had planted many of the trees in the Wolseley neighbourhood of Winnipeg. From Ariel I learned that Mary Ann was credited with planting the famous Wolseley Elm, a much-disputed tree in the middle of a main thoroughfare once named the smallest park in the world by *Ripley's Believe It or Not!*™. Planted before Confederation, "It was inconvenient, but … had become a symbol to Winnipeggers." I do not know if my father knew about this, but I do recall him taking me to an old wooden Anglican church outside of Portage la Prairie where he showed me the graves of our Ancestors. At that time, he told me that he was pretty sure we were related to the Goods. He was not one to talk about being Métis, so he surprised me when he said someone in our family, he couldn't recall who, had letters from Louis Riel. That was in 2010. After taking me there, he returned to his quiet self. To this day we know very little about his life or what he knew about our ancestry.

After one month of making space for our new home, I am stunned by how dark my father is. Maybe he has been hiding from the sun, just as he has always hidden the tattoos that are above his knees. When wearing shorts or swimming trunks, he puts Band-Aids over the tattoos. Mom says he got them while he was in the navy. No one knows what they are. Could be a picture, a word … another woman's name?

By now I know that being fairer skinned is important to both of my parents. I know this because I tan "too easily," and it has been mentioned more than once. One such discussion ended with my mom ordering whitening cream. That was in Goose Bay, where everything had to be airlifted in. Just think, the preferred skin colour could be flown in … from where? I have no idea, but I understand there are still people whitening their skin.

As I learned more about the history of the Métis People, I began to wonder if my father's pull to Charleswood and my love of kâtêpwêwisîpiy, the Assiniboine River, wasn't somehow connected to our Ancestors. Charleswood was the location of "The Passage." Found at the end of Berkley Street, this was where the river was at its lowest. According to the noted historian of the Métis People Lawrence J. Barkwell, it was a natural ford where the buffalo and the Red River carts could easily cross:

> The Passage was frequently used by Métis buffalo hunters travelling to Pembina, and independent traders wanting to bypass the Forks in defiance of the H.B.C.'s monopoly.

A few years ago, I drove by that old house and saw the yard filled with the trees my dad had saved from the contractors. The house is a simple house, one of those split-levels that were so popular then. It was the cheapest house available, a two-bedroom, one-bathroom, with a basement partially above ground. The three boys had to sleep in the unfinished basement. Dad was going to make bedrooms down there but only got as far as the framing before Gordon drowned.

Every time someone died, we moved.

BORN OF WATER

*The wild, the romantic song of the voyageurs, as they
plied their brisk paddles, struck upon my ear ... with
hearts joyful ... [they] sang, with all the force of
three hundred manly voices.*

—R.M. BALLANTYNE

Hudson's Bay: or, Every-Day Life in the Wilds of North
America: during Six Years' Residence in the Territories
of the Honourable Hudson's Bay Company (1848)

born of water
meant to float
I sink until I rise
to the big sky songs
of my people travelling rivers
strong arms paddling

    one stroke per second

my Ancestors' canoes carried them north
where a daughter was born
the mixing of blood continued until

    I born of water

give thanks   hold my hands up

    to the big sky

rolling back west I kneel
before the mountains
sit by an ocean of words
my place uncertain until

    I born of water

hear the songs

    of the Métis voyageurs

paddling

    one stroke per second

UNTETHERED

is it my blood that makes me wander?
the diaspora of my soul   scattered
over many lands
the bones of my Ancestors
how they pull on me   offering so many directions
yet how can I answer the many folded inside my body?

this body not my own   a shared place of suffering

       it searches for safety

looks for a cord tying me to you ... and you and you
yet soon we will all leave this room
leave each other   it is then that I will feel
how alone I am   in the Territory of the Salish
with the bones of my Ancestors

       scattered over many lands

some just north of here
Fort St. James the place where many lay
others can be found at Turtle Mountain, the Prairies
L'Anse aux Meadows, and Iceland
as I trace their steps I feel them beside me   whispering

      look here – comes another voice – *no here!*

their stories forgotten   they ask me to sing home their bones
to find them in the stories of our people
they ask me to tether myself to them and to the stories
a chain unbroken   we are stronger
the stories of those that came before the link

      untethered we are lost

but if we are patient in our searching
we may find a way out
of this place of loss
out of the wandering
that comes when one does not know
the stories of their Ancestors

TELL ME AGAIN

tell me again about the days
before buffalo bones became china
about the days when rivers were roadways
tell me again about the days before
the white man's timekeeping ways

Are We Cursed?
Looking Back

Unresolved grief is like a low-grade fever.

—STEPHEN LEVINE

*Unattended Sorrow: Recovering from Loss
and Reviving the Heart* (2005)

We can't find my brother Gordon. He has gone missing while canoeing on kâtêpwêwisîpiy, the Assiniboine River. That night I dream of him ringing the doorbell and when I open our front door he is there, dripping wet. He is laughing, says, "I was just playing a trick on everyone."

The next day they drag the river. My dad is there when they find him, tangled in the woody debris that has accumulated at the bottom of the river.

Since his birth, when I was two, he has been my closest friend. When little we played house. We wanted to marry one another.

He loved to pretend he was just home from work, opening my bedroom door, saying, "Honey, I'm home."

Now he is never coming home.

⁓

The Assiniboine Park gates are closed but it is easy to go around them. I have done it many times, late at night, whenever the river called to me. Now this river, the one where I shared my first kiss with my high-school sweetheart, has betrayed me. I feel the need to confront it.

Drunk and alone in the middle of the night during flood season, I make my way to the edge of the rushing water, shouting, "Why? Why? Why ... take my brother?"

The fast-moving water drowns out my voice as I slide in the mud, moving ever closer to the turbulence that is water.

I am in danger, but I do not care. I am contemplating letting the river take me. I want to join my sweet brother.

Four years later, I lie on the grave of my second brother, Murray.

Once again it's the middle of the night and I'm drunk. I have broken into the cemetery where he and Gordon are buried. This time I have an accomplice. I needed someone to drive me there. My dear husband, Paul, has no idea what to do with me. No one does. They try, but I am unreachable.

I begin to think that we Kirtons are cursed, and that everyone should be advised to stay away from us.

I move back home. I need to be with what is left of our family.

My youngest brother, Robert, is just ten years old. He has always been such a blessing to our family. Without him it would just be the three of us now. Mom, Dad, and me. A nice little triangle.

My parents bought a new house after Gordon drowned. They now live in a quaint farmhouse that sits on five acres on the aptly named Liberty Street: We are, after all, in need of liberation.

I can feel Murray here. I do still love my husband Paul, but maybe his mother was right. She never wanted us to marry. We were just eighteen, and next to his "normal" family, mine looked all the more dysfunctional.

I belong here, in this home, with these people and our ghosts.

Each day after work I sit at the dinner table. My food made salty by tears, I cannot eat. The doctor says I have the beginnings of an ulcer; he is concerned.

I have little to say to anyone. All I have to offer is tears. When I cry, my father scowls, asks my mother, "What is wrong with her?"

Late at night, most nights, my dad sits drunk in the kitchen spitting his words. I hear him talking to my mother. It's always "she" did this or "she" did that.

He never says my name.

Worse yet, in his opinion, I am a bad influence on my one remaining brother.

~

Murray visits me in my sleep. I feel the weight of his head heavy on my chest. I touch his thick, curly hair and hear him say, "I was too young ... too young to die." He is still here in this house.

I am not ready to leave him.

There is already talk of selling this house and moving into a townhouse. I can stay until then. Or can I?

~

I wake to the sound of screaming, my mom running into my bedroom. She is frantic, trying to hide between the wall and my single bed. My father is close behind. Soon his arms are over my head reaching for her throat.

I sit up and push him away. She runs out the door. Now I am alone with him and he turns his rage towards me.

~

I am in and out of consciousness, slumping down the wall as he punches me hard in the face. It's not the first time.

Years later, after many sinus infections, I see an ENT doctor. "Your nose is a mess. What happened to you?" I tell him all I can think of is a car accident at twenty-one. "I hit the steering wheel. Thirty-five stitches. I needed thirty-five stitches and lost my front teeth." He says, it is worse than that. He shakes his head, says, "Your nose has been broken many times. You will need surgery."

The night after that surgery, lying alone in my hospital bed, I remember.

Remembering hurts.

~

"Am I going to die? Will he kill me this time?"

I do not know how, but somehow I manage to push him out of the room and thankfully there is a lock on the door and a phone in the room.

I call 911 and wait.

Where is my mother? Is she okay? Why did she leave me alone with him?

~

As I head downstairs to check on my mother, I am in shock, forget that the police are on their way. When they do arrive, my father has his hands around my throat. He is strangling me in the kitchen. My nose is bloody, my lip split. I have a goose egg on my forehead, another on my cheek, my whole face is swollen.

The police never speak to me. I'm twenty-two and small; in my flannel nightgown, I look younger than I am. My mother reassures them that everything is okay.

They leave.

Years later I remember all the times my dad cautioned me, saying he knew who I hung out with. At that time I had found new friends, many from the North End, some from Tuxedo. The rich liked to party with us. My dad tells me often, "I know all the police officers. I drink with them. They are my friends." He tells me he knows who I hang out with.

~

I cannot stay here; it is not safe. I pack my things into my car, drive to my ex-husband's. Once there, he lays me on the couch, gets ice, and sits next to me, crying.

I ask to come home, but he says, "No. I want you. I really do ... but not like this."

The truth of these words stings.

~

The next day, I call in sick and make the mistake of telling my manager what has happened. I will need a new home, so begin an apartment search without a job, as she fired me. I "have too many problems," she says, "it is all too much."

I am alone. Jobless and homeless.

At least I have a car.

I have friends and maybe I can go back to my old job, but first I have to heal my face. I mean, really, who would rent to someone who looks like they just lost a boxing match?

Who would hire me?

~

I am once again banned from my parents' home. My mother is not to see me or talk to me. I am not allowed to see or talk to my baby brother. I am to be blamed for what happened. "If only you weren't so difficult."

~

After a long and tiring search, I finally find an affordable apartment on Corydon Avenue. I have never lived alone and am afraid. It is an old building and mostly empty, as they just renovated. With very few residents, the building feels oddly hollow. This only heightens my senses.

I can feel the ghostly presence of past tenants. The haunted hollowing-out of hallways and suites mirrors how I feel inside.

The building manager puts me in the suite next to his. An aging womanizer, he wants to keep an eye on me. He likes to come hang out with me in my apartment, and when he does, he tells me about his life as a gigolo.

He is much older than me. I don't want him the way he wants me. But I need him.

~

Every night I go to bars where I find men to buy me the drinks I can't afford. I miss my husband and occasionally we run into one another. Sometimes we go home together until he finds a girlfriend, a woman he later marries.

~

There are frequent visits from the building manager. On one of these occasions, he stands in my kitchen reeking of sex, which I try to ignore. He tells me he is concerned and asks if I am okay. He says that when I come home from the bar, I cry loudly enough for him to hear me. Vague remembrances of wailing pass through my mind. I am too embarrassed to tell him that I drink so much and sleep around because I want to disappear. I laugh it off. I tell no one that I want to die, not even my mother.

———

Over the years there was always some man offering to save me. Most simply handed me their dick as I took their hand believing they really wanted to help. I soon learned no man was going to save me. I had to save myself.

———

It would be some time before I understood what colonization had done to my family. Not just my father struggled. His mother and his siblings did as well. They tried, though. Grandma Rose was renowned for the wedding gowns she made. An entrepreneur, she took care of her children by herself after my Métis grandfather fell off a grain elevator and died, leaving her alone with four small children. She told me once that she made my step-grandfather, Fred the fireman, wait to marry her. She said, "I didn't want anyone else raising my children."

As a young girl, Grandma Rose had been left with other families after her own mother died of smallpox. She attended Catholic day school, and somewhere along the line, she left behind her language and her culture.

A sophisticated woman, she could be hard to reach. Her time at the Brandon Mental Institute, the shock treatment and medications for depression, left her dry-mouthed and inaccessible. When I was young, I was afraid I would end up like her. Sadly, the thing I was most afraid of was looking like her.

Her daughters, my aunts Val and Eileen, both married white men. Grandma Rose's second husband, Fred, was also a white man.

Everyone was invested in what some call "respectability politics." How we looked was a priority. No matter their income level, most of the women wore red lipstick, dressed fashionably, and had the latest hairstyles. Their outfits often included hats and gloves. Grandma could make anything. She used her skills as a seamstress to make them all presentable.

What always confused me was the white powder they would use on their faces. It was clearly several shades lighter than their actual skin colour. Even though it was never fully articulated, I was receiving the message, "White is best." My father and his brother, my uncle Gordie, both married white women. Perhaps they all wanted fairer children, but some of us were not so white. DNA is like that. You never know what you're going to get in the genetic game of life.

———

Many of my Métis cousins have stories of abuse and neglect. We all lived with the fractures and the pain our parents, grandparents, and great-grandparents passed along to us. Innocent vessels, we floated through life, mimicking what we thought would bring success. And yes, there was some success, but there was always sabotage lurking within the shame we carried. None of us knew the shame was not ours. None of us knew what had happened to our Ancestors. We didn't even know we were Métis. That and many other things was kept from us.

Regardless of our troubles, there was always lots of love and laughter. It was in the homes of my Métis relatives that I felt most myself.

I AM

I am the daughter of a shape-shifter
a loon weeping in the night
casting spells on all who listen

I am the daughter of a shape-shifter
a black-billed magpie following
waiting for scraps from buffalo hunts

I am the daughter of a shape-shifter
building a mud dome near the ocean
most days I hide there until night

I am the daughter of a shape-shifter
thrice burned   thrice reborn

    I avoid the light

DIRTY

i

some words stay with you
live just below
the skin
present themselves
here and there
in speech patterns
a stumbling on
certain words
a holding of body (hostage)
a body that signals stay
then stay away

                                        stay away
                                    for I am dirty

ii

my father showered three times a day
obsessed with the polishing
of his shoes
my mother
obsessed with the polishing
of floors   hardwood must shine
hair and makeup offered as camouflage
a way to hide in the trees with marriage
where, if lucky   one could find love
if not, he has money you don't have and

        he is handsome

iii

shoes polished
he sweeps her
off her feet
until there is me
I am dirty

brown   unexpected girl
not boy who can polish his shoes
don skates   push firm
just push   Momma just pushed
me out   no one was happy
that I was a girl
that I was brown
everyone just kept pushing
polishing   whitening
cream but one method
of eliminating fear
moving it from their bodies
to mine   polishing an abrasion
on my skin   whitening
cream intended to soothe everyone

                    but me

QUIETLY DROWNING

for Gordon
December 15, 1956–July 8, 1973

unable to call for help
you silently sank

your drowning a cascading event
sent us all down the rapids without a canoe
each separated by the currents of alcohol

we tumbled
                    over sharp rocks of grief

our mother crying out as we headed to bars
where the jukebox said things we could not

our mother crying as ...

                    I take the ribbon from my hair

lay with men who never make rose garden promises
strangers willing to help me make it until morning's light

when what I really wanted
was for you to be sixteen in our kitchen
so happy about that new job

when what I really wanted was
to go back to the day you left
to say   I love you

as you headed out the door

        how was I to know

                    you would never return

HOPE LOST

for Murray
July 2, 1958–September 2, 1977

I still find it hard to speak of you
you had a temper my boy
fists always ready for a fight
your wiry body wound tight

I was four when you were born
into a family on the edge of extinction
our buffalo-blooded ways in your bones
when I think of you I can feel the French
the Métis and the pain of displacement

our shared history a bond
a burden made light by love
in you I saw a fire I could return to
I saw hope and truly believed
one death per family is enough
that Gordon would want us to carry on

it was me dear brother who asked Dad to call you
it was me who told him to say
you could come home
it was me dear brother who asked Dad to call you
and when he did his brother took you in
it was there that a bullet landed in you

your death leaving me without hope
our shared history still binds us together
it was me dear brother

                    it was me …

FAIR GAME

buffalo bones lay remembering
the way you took it all
your never-enough ways held danger
manifested as men on horses with guns
considered fair game when really
what is fair about a contest
between men on horses with guns
and a lumbering beast
whose running only ended over a cliff
where they all lay dying slowly

        until there were no more

WHAT ARE YOU, ANYWAY?

When we keep these men's secrets, we allow their
predatory behaviour to thrive.

—ROXANE GAY

"Roxane Gay, Aimee Bender, and More on
Assault and Harassment in the Literary World:
11 Women Writers in Response to Bonnie
Nadzam's Essay, 'Experts in the Field'" (2017)

his *what are you, anyway* fingers creep
up my sheer blouse
hands seeking flesh   loosen
grip of camisole meant
to screen out prying eyes and soon
his roughness a stain on my blouse
his skin on my skin considered polite discourse
a way to get to know one another
I cringe inside   smile outside

no one told me to expect this
yet they must have known
his hungry eyes that wander
to girls in blouses and the pencil skirts
intended to make us professional

our appearance a balancing of between
cautioned against the matronly look
of the midi and away from the mini
our availability measured in skirt lengths monitored
by fathers who may also be bank managers seeking solace
in exotic others as his *what are you, anyway* fingers
creep up her sheer blouse
how is it that the territory of our flesh
remains his mountain to climb and once done
we are left to pick the bones of those who went before us

MADE MAD

(inspired by the 1963 movie *The Haunting*)

her body an evil house   a haunting on a hill
where men enter gaping doorways
opened by magic and pills

some say she was made mad by death
she had always hoped to slip through
the cracks one day
to be herself or someone similar

her strong instinct for preservation   not enough
she stole the family car   became part
of an experiment where the maid leaves before dark

it always felt like the darkness wanted her
the spiral staircase death threats
the feel of metal steps swirling around her

she often wondered if she had
the requisite skill set
her toolbox tricks untested

they had a common interest
he suggested she think about it
she had hoped not to need him

but her body betrayed her

       if only she had somewhere to go

A Fresh Start:
One Door Closes,
Another Opens

The old instinct had always been to gather the
feelings and opinions [about the trauma] that were
scattered through the village, to gather them like
willow twigs and tie them into a single prayer bundle
that would bring peace to all of them. But now the
feelings were twisted, tangled roots, and all the names
for the source of this growth were buried ... out of
reach. And there would be no peace and the people
would have no rest until the entanglement had been
unwound to the source.

—LESLIE MARMON SILKO
Ceremony (1977)

Six months sober, I request a transfer from the Edmonton
Airport to the Canadian Airlines reservations office in downtown
Vancouver. Once again I look for an affordable apartment, but it
is not easy. Expo 86 was just last year. Vancouver had invited the
world; many stayed, driving rents up and availability down. I am
still a new employee, so my hourly wage is low. Now that I am full-
time at the airline, I won't be able to work part-time at the bank
like I had been doing in Edmonton.

I know that it will be hard, but I am once again in need of a fresh
start. Newly divorced from my second husband, I have left behind
a home that was never considered mine. I ask nothing of my
husband. I knew going in that he considered everything his. But
at least I am free of suburbia, a place I had run to thinking I could
change my life, only to find I was making "a geographical cure."

I move into an apartment that does not have screens on the
windows. I spend time opening and closing the hinged windows;
I lean out, smell the moist air. Coming from the prairies, where
mosquitoes ruled, where the air was so dry that it sometimes hurt
your nostrils, this is a wonder to me.

I go to AA meetings daily. Frequently I consider various forms of self-harm. Sometimes I give in, especially late at night after my father calls drunk and feeling the need to remind me that I am a slut.

I am thirty-two years old, and my sponsor has to tell me that I don't have to answer the phone.

~

I find a friend with a history worse than mine. We decide to co-sponsor each other. But it is not enough.

When alone, I hear my dead mother crying out for my help. Sometimes I hear my father, his anger exploding over anyone in his way. His voice comes from behind, like being hit in the back of the head. Hers comes from the earth, mirroring the growling and guttural fear that took hold in our bodies when Father was angry. Sobriety is revealing all the cracks. There is nowhere to hide.

~

I check myself into the Maple Ridge Treatment Centre. I am there not because I want to drink but rather because most days I want to die. I am anxious all the time.

~

In group therapy I share how spiritual I am. The therapist takes a deep breath and says, "But you want to die. You do know what it means to be spiritual ... don't you?" I think I do, but now I am not sure. My carefully constructed persona may have some fault lines, but I am not ready to admit this. I long for invisibility. I want him to move on to his next victim, but he is not done with me yet. He tells me that his understanding of the word is that it means "to have an enthusiasm for life." This I do not have. I want to die. I am anxious all the time. Even so I am undeterred, and every morning I get up and do my hair and makeup. I then choose one of the many fancy track suits I purchased on credit to wear while in treatment. I am engaged to be married, but heck, there are lots of broken men here, some handsome. I did always like to have one on the shelf. Just in case.

~

Each day we have group therapy. I am learning to tell my story, and in my story I am a victim, not the predator. After a week of this, the therapist says, "You scare me." He is not buying my victim status. I could try to argue with him. I have plenty of stories in which I am the victim, but this is AA. I am to keep my side of the sidewalk clean, and besides, I do know why he says that. I recall my one-night-stand disco days and how I had made the decision to never marry again. I would instead have rotating boyfriends, preferably with cabins at Lake of the Woods. My time in the disco had taught me that when it came to men and women, someone was going to be used, and it wasn't going to be me. I decided to hunt men, to be in charge. It would be some time before I would see the flaws in that plan. While I was using them, they were also using me, and they were better at it.

———

I have made a new friend. She Who Saved Me is a fiery Black woman who speaks her mind. She has seen the way I do my hair and makeup every day and all those matching track suits. My second week there, at breakfast, she reaches across the table, holds my hand and says, "You do know you're in treatment, don't you?" She can see through me, wants to help me. The mixed-message queen that I am is wanting to look good while wanting to die, while hunting men, while being the most spiritual person in the room. She has my number. We are fast friends, both of us with difficult childhoods and connections to Winnipeg. Years later I name my son after her grandmother.

———

I am to take my inventory, do a Step Four, to find my character flaws. There are many, but I have already done a Step Four in the past, so decide I should just focus on sex and men this time. I write pages and pages of stories about my time with men. All the men I have had sex with, some unnamed as I don't always recall their names. Some I owe an apology. Some owe me one. There was rape, over and over again. Drunk women in bars are easy prey, and women who claim sexual agency are seen to have given up the right to say "No" to anyone.

———

I sit across the table from a small, kind man in a black robe and white collar. I read my Step Four without looking up. I barely take a breath as I machine-gun through all the stories of all the men, my time in nightclubs and after-hours clubs in search of relief from all that haunted me. I have never told anyone some of this stuff. Once done, I look up to see his expressionless face and then I hear him say, "You know nothing about love." This offered simply as an observation, no judgment, no pity. I know he is right. I know what he has said is important. Even so, I have no idea what to do. I go home to my sober, biker boyfriend and try for "normal." We both join CoDA (Co-Dependents Anonymous). I return to my therapist.

My therapist tells me I have the most severely altered baseline for abuse she has ever seen. She sends me home with a list. It is to help me know what abusive behaviour is. Clearly I need it if I had to be told I didn't have to take my father's late-night drunken, abusive phone calls.

Soon I am enrolled in a survivor's group with other victims of child predators. My therapist is convinced that I have been sexually abused. I have no memory of this, but she says I have all the signs, and there are dreams that seem to indicate she is right. To this day nothing has been confirmed, my memory banks were wiped clean, and all data appears to be unretrievable. For a time I considered hypnotherapy but, in the end, decide if it isn't coming naturally, maybe it is not true, maybe it was planted there by the therapist. Goddess, I hope so.

In the first session of our survivor's group, I shake uncontrollably as a woman speaks about the things her father did to her and how one day her mother saw them in bed together. For an instant she thought, "Now I'm safe ..." but her mother turned around and tiptoed out of the room, carefully closing the door behind her.

I am learning that other mothers did not protect their daughters. This information is too much for me to take in. The reverberations of this knowledge cause my body to vibrate. I can't hold my coffee cup. The group therapist advises me to go to the UBC Psych. Ward, where I am given drugs. Once home, anti-anxiety pills in hand, I call my sponsor, who instructs me to flush them down the toilet. Apparently she feels there are no shortcuts to sanity. I agree to do so and then spend the next five years wondering if I made the right decision.

My therapist says, "You have chronic shock," which we now call PTSD. It has left me with memory deficits. I cannot remember what any of my bedrooms looked like. I feel disconnected from my own story. When reporting on my own life, I am more visitor/observer than participant.

She tells me to ask my relatives what they knew. My aunt Joyce says she remembers coming to visit us when I was thirteen. She says, "You just sat on the steps, in the hallway, while everyone was in the living room, your skin erupting in fiery-red eczema." I tell my auntie that my mother didn't like to take us to the doctor, that my hands were frequently infected. That my mom would say things like, "We really shouldn't bother the nice doctors with that." My aunt Joyce says, "I could see you were in trouble, but what could I do?"

My therapist suggests I go home to Winnipeg and visit my old haunts. I need to retrieve my story, my spirit, and to see if more memories will come if I visit the people and places I once knew. I book a flight to Winnipeg. I go to my junior high, walk down the halls. Nothing feels familiar. I do not recall being there.

I leave confused, walk the path to our old home. The dirt remembers me. I can feel the ruts of my long-ago steps. Once at the corner of Dieppe and Coventry Roads, a memory surfaces. I know this corner and the small house where a small boy lived. I never knew his name, but I recall the day he stood on the corner crying. I had stopped to ask if he was okay. He told me his mother had died. A piece of him is still there, and me, witnessing. The moment imprinted on the pavement.

I still wish I knew what to say to him.

I carry on. Head to the house that made us homeowners, not renters. This was to be where everything would change for us.

I can hear the reverberations of my mother's screams. See her chasing those two women my dad had brought home from the bar. It feels so real that for a second I worry what the neighbours might think. The things they must have seen. I remember their kindness when Gordon died. All those casseroles delivered, and Mom crying in the kitchen.

I see now that we were doomed, but I did not know why. I did not know about colonization or what my father and mother had endured. I did not know about epigenetics or intergenerational trauma. Instead, I wondered if we were cursed.

NIBBLES

I have been feeding on my own body
it began with my toes
surely no one will know
this I can hide

just one toe   the big one
it was only meant to pacify but soon
there were urges to nibble just a little
small bites   the way a lover
might nip at your neck
not too hard   just enough
to bring electricity to the skin
just enough to remove numbness

over time I needed more
the bites became blood sport
teeth marks I can hide inside my shoes

like the snake swallowing its tail
I am becoming a circular version of myself

when in public I bite my baby finger
I have found that I can disappear
into the throbbing of digits
like the snake swallowing her tail
I am becoming a circular version of myself

MEMORIES

there was a time I wanted to remember
I considered hypnotherapy
while rejecting the dreams
that came in the night

> I am a small child, a girl
> I am the girl and I am an observer
> I sit on a couch and watch as I
> a young girl in a short white dress
> bend over to pick up a doll
> frilly panties flashing vulnerability
> the one that observes tries to scream
> nothing comes out

> I know there are others with us
> one cannot be trusted
> I do not want him to see
> my three-year-old self bending over

> I do not want him to see my frilly panties
> my little white socks with lace
> I cannot scream and wonder why
> no one else can see the danger

more dreams come   some recurring

> I am in the kitchen
> a teenager
> holding back tears
> as my father's fists
> pound the table

> there is a dog
> with a sharp tongue
> between my legs

> I am to say nothing

there was a time I wanted to remember

SEXISM 101

every night there is a shouting
in my ear
a ringing going out
a circular sound sent far by force
a slap across the head
I am hurled forward hoping
to avoid what comes next

"You little slut"

shouted at my tiny body
one that has not known sex
but is accused of time with boys
yet when the neighbour complains
about my younger brother
playing doctor with their daughter
my father nods   appears to agree

until the door closes and
he high-fives my brother

ANXIETY

with no one to tell
I develop strategies

                              stare at a photo
                         disappear into fuchsia
                              count backwards
                             from one hundred
                                 over and over

when driving decipher
licence plates
alpha bravo six

                                    landlocked
                                I long to float
                              find ways around
                                all I cannot say

PREDISPOSED

this small child could be me
her uncle an island of profanity
drunk on women's bodies
he cannot see her innocence

all those years spent aligning my chakras
as the losses piled themselves at my door
and the men in my family stood guard

there were reputations to protect
and we were women
delicate as butterflies pinned to a wall
our despair drifting between us

but now my breasts are doing the downward dog
withering cleavage evidence of the fading
orbiting the unsayable
I can see I still know so little
that I am still making my way
towards the knowledge
that all that came next was set in motion
by one who could not see   who still cannot see

this small child could be me

                    was me

HUNGRY

innocent and yet not
playing manipulation mind games

we hunted one another
in bars where we all satiated

our longing
for flesh-filled promises

making each other prey
until one of us lost themselves

in the struggle for satisfaction
and the other declared victory by moving on

to the next foolish girl or boy

it is true I never won

                    or did I?

once a foolish girl
innocent and yet not

erupting shame   emitting "pick me" signals
skin exploding eczema red

puss-filled evidence that fear lives here
has made a home in my body

exploding outward
until I learn my flesh is sacred

until I declare victory
my body a sovereign nation

Rebirth: We All Come from Somewhere

If a woman has a collapsing mother, she must refuse to become one herself.

—CLARISSA PINKOLA ESTÉS, PH.D.

Women Who Run with the Wolves: Myths and Stories of the Wild Woman Archetype (1992)

I was to be a childless woman. Having watched the women in my life, especially my mother, I knew that having children made you vulnerable. This feeling heightened when in my second marriage I became pregnant. I gave thanks that it was an ectopic pregnancy, one that left me writhing in pain on my couch for a full day. Having been taught by my mother to "not bother the nice doctors," I waited twelve hours for my husband to come home from work. Once home, he didn't even stop to shower, as it was clear I needed to be rushed to emergency. The doctors were shocked. They said I should have come sooner. There may have been damage. They would know more after the surgery.

That night, lyng alone in my hospital bed, I had many thoughts. There was some relief, as having a child with my second husband could end badly. But there was something more ominous lurking in my mind. That curse was there and the very old feeling that something was wrong with me *down there*, as I referred to it in those days. My womanliness had been compromised by some earlier event. I decided once again I was not to have children, but years later She Who Saved Me, my dear friend, the one from treatment, told me that a child showed up in my astrology chart. They would be born in 1990 or 1991.

I thought she had to be wrong. I was certain that I was not meant to be a mother. Turns out what they say about our biological clocks and the way that some women reach a certain age and suddenly want to be a mother was true for me. I remember when, at thirty-three, I began to consider you.

The first time I met you I was lying on the couch of Vijay, a healer specializing in a healing practice called "rebirthing." For months now she has been taking me back to my own birth. Sometimes we do this in water to make it easier for me to enter the spaces where I began. Together we visit my mother's womb, a time before words. In those moments all that exists is water and the drumbeat of my mother's heart.

Every visit, Vijay asks me to recall my descent down the birth canal. Some days I resist the best way I know how: I escape into my mind, the wordless place of meditation. When she notices this has happened, she asks me to change position, to get on the floor on all fours. I am to breathe deeply, pump my body up and down. I don't like this. I prefer the drifting. Then one day while floating on her couch, there you were touching my face as a blind person reads Braille. My face a map you followed. Your hands I now know. I could feel your spirit, the lightness of it, of you, as you introduced yourself to me.

Perhaps a husband is the problem, not the child. Perhaps one day I will do this on my own. Well, not totally on my own, but you know what I mean. My grandma Rose raised four children after her husband died. She did this because she did not trust another man with her children. If she could do it, so can I.

A year later, my body full of life, you presented yourself again, this time in a dream. Restless that night as your fingers and toes pressed against my ribs until they ached, I entered sleep only to find I can see you in the liminal space of the dream world. I feel your outstretched hands push against the skin of my hard belly. They feel familiar. I feel your desire to be released. I see the outline of your face pushing against my swollen belly announcing your arrival. I see you. You are here.

My sweet boy – I am considering names for you. Names that
my brother says will follow you. "Why can't he just be Jordan
or Jessie?" I realize my brother is right and that although this
is my moment to be creative, I do need to think of how names
create realities. Jessie does sound nice. I like the way it feels in my
mouth and you do feel like a Jessie. For a middle name why not
Lane? You are named after my dear friend's Black grandmother, a
woman I never met but felt like I knew. For years now, I have been
listening to stories about the big-hearted woman, Jessie Lane, the
one who raised my friend after she was left alone, as a small baby,
in a hotel room.

I will never leave you alone in a hotel room. I am a sober mom. I
have a good job. All is well. Or so I think.

Now twenty-nine, my son is in therapy. He calls me nearly every
day, asks me if I have read this book or that book. He is unpacking
his early years and the fact that he has only seen his father once.
That was just a few years ago, when he decided to just fly up to
Haida Gwaii and present himself to the man who has frequently
promised to call when in town. My son does not know that I
destroyed all the court documents or that I feel guilty for leaving
the father's name blank on his birth certificate. When he was born,
I was not sure who the father was. Understandably, his father felt
DNA testing was necessary; there had been innocent movement
from one lover to another when I had thought Mike and I were
done. But he begged me back with promises of love and marriage,
a life in what we called "the Charlottes" in those days. That
promise opened me, and my body said "Yes!" to this child, only to
say "No!" to staying with his father who was already backtracking.

The night before a judge is to determine child support, I receive
a call asking me to accept one third of what will no doubt be
ordered the next day. Within this offer to settle out of court is a
poison pill: a threat to never see Jessie if I don't accept. Mike says

it will be easier for him to forget, to forgive, if I do this. Against the wishes of my lawyer, I agree.

I wish I had known he would not fulfill his end, that the first visit to Haida Gwaii, when Jessie was three months old, would be the last. I wish I had known that his father would say, "That can't be my baby. He is too dark." I wish I had known there were science deniers even then. 99.6 percent proof of parentage was not enough.

But most of all, I wish I had known how to be a better mother.

UMBILICAL

i

a navel string
connecting us
delivering sustenance
until shock of light awakens me
doctors, nurses in masks surround
sound words delivered

it's a girl

ii

liquid-born I linger
on the edge of what I know
about my mother
the way she held me
within her womb

I have wondered
did she want me?

I do recall her saying:

the best days of my life were
the days my children were born

tied to us she could not leave

iii

first-born
the only girl
I held potential
egg-filled promises of love
delivered faulty fetuses
until one managed to hold on

iv

my son I wanted a water birth for you
no shock of light or masked faces
I wanted to welcome you
but once you arrived I could not hold you
arms, knees shaking I vibrated loss
mourned the absence of water
the crooked path down a canal too narrow

I give thanks that you made it, son
now that you are here, and I am alone
ghosts linger, nibble on your toes
whisper in my ear reminding me
of my mother's words
my mother's love
she too is glad you are here

SAMSĀRA

i

Mother I have lost my place
it is dark here Mother
without you
the earth is damp
made thin by loss I am cold
in need of shelter

ii

I have a son now Mother
he swims within me
I must build a fire
light the way for your return

iii

he cautions me in the kitchen when I am angry
his small finger pointing
he says   "I used to be your mother!"

iv

I hear a cry
he has touched a hot iron
his lips pouting, he has that
why-would-that-thing-want-to-hurt-me look
I scoop him up, rush to the rocking chair
where I cradle him while he cries
then pauses just once to say
"your mother never did this, did she?"

how does he know this?
was he a toddler remembering another life?
I don't know, but he was always reminding me
that he is not just a child, that the wheel turns

FOR JESSIE

that first morning I woke to you beside me
your old man face and tiny body
you asleep inside a transparent crib

        my first thought

            you are real

my belly distended had contained life
held you as you swam outstretched
fingers and toes poking my ribs until they ached
even so my womb was a welcoming place

           and now you are here

I never told you I was afraid
my first day home alone with you
a stranger who knows my body
cries for the milk I do not produce enough of

        I had no idea how to care for you

you were always hungry my boy
and I the vigilant mother
would sit all night in that rocking chair
a plate of food beside me

        Om Namah Shivaya on repeat

just you and I sitting in moonlight
with the need for nourishment
I prayed   you cried   I prayed
until my breasts became a prayer

        while you unaware slept in my arms

WHAT LIES BENEATH

I am potential on a precipice
body leaning into wind
I plunge into an ocean
feel salt in mouth
breathe underwater
until awakened
by thoughts
of all I have to do

the tension between
what you need son
and what I can do
brings pressure
the need for air
heavy it comes whispering

         every night

BROKEN WINDOWS

why is it that we push the forlorn to the fringe?
their broken-window stares reminding us
that there is a place of between
a place of here and now
yet not here   not now

we want to believe it could never happen to us
our strong bodies safe in suburbia
where mothers can protect their children
walk grocery store aisles
where all manner of food can be found

we cannot think of the hungry
their broken-window stares
we need to believe it could never happen to us

              until it does

                   and if it does

despair will enter the room
there will be tears   hungry children
falling through our fingers
knowing we cannot save them
we will be left to wander
the empty rooms of what was

our broken-window stares
turning even the kindhearted away

Hungry: Hurt People Hurt People

It's a hungry, hungry world
Don't let them devour you whole.

—RISING APPALACHIA
"Hungry World" (2021)

Eight and a half years sober, the mother of a glowing three-year-old, I am a spiritual seeker. Believing I have awakened and maybe one day will ascend, I often think I could be good at this game. But something always holds me back. I like to think it was the Ancestors whispering in my ear saying things like "Timing is everything," but knowing my family, it was probably them poking me in the ribs and laughing while saying, "Get over yourself, you foolish girl."

~

I sign up for a business administration diploma at Sprott Shaw College. I have plans. I am going to bring light into workplaces as a "bring your soul to work" consultant.

I have begun to see that I do need a partner, a father for my three-year-old son. He will need to be a healer, too.

I find him and at first do not recognize him. But he has seen me. He has been watching me.

~

The first time he sits next to me in business school, I can feel his interest, but I write it off, as he is clearly much younger than me. He is persistent – a trait I would later learn to fear.

~

We have been paired off by the instructor. There is an assignment to complete, but Dean is nowhere to be seen, so I head to the computer lab to do some research. Halfway through this study session he arrives wafting Boss cologne. He is the boss, and I am floating in the scent of him; then he creates a bubble of energy around us. This is not my first time in the presence of a master. I know how they can fill rooms with bliss, but never have I seen this done in daylight, in a professional setting. I look around and no one else seems to notice. He winks at me. Every cell in my body is fluttering in the breeze of his presence.

～

That night, in my sleep, he visits. Dreaming and yet awake, I feel him hovering over me. He enters me and we merge in the kind of lovemaking I have been dreaming of for years now. Even so, I am angry. Where was the consent?

～

At school the next day I look for him and when I find him blurt out, "How dare you come to me in the night like that?" Surprised that I was aware of his presence in the dreamworld, he laughs, not at me, but more with delight which he tries to hide. I have seen that same look on my father's face when I outdid the boys in any activity. I could see he was pleased but did not want to encourage my budding independence.

Dean tells me that he has been watching me for months. He knows who I travel with. He asks me to go downstairs to the café for coffee. Once there he tells me that he is an awake dreamer, an astral traveller, and a remote viewer. He says his specialty is women. When I tell him that I am a single mom and training at Battered Women's Support Services, he repeats his specialty is women.

～

I am beginning to soften towards him. Perhaps he is an angel. He is clearly a healer. If I am ever to become that enlightened healer, don't I need a partner like this?

He asks me to go for a drink, but I don't drink. I don't say this. I say yes.

～

I feel my hand on the railing as I make my descent down the stairs. I have not been in a bar in many years. It does not hold the appeal it once did; all that clinking of glasses and the smell of beer is no longer the call I respond to.

For many years now I have burned incense, Nag Champa, when I meditate daily. Throughout the day I live in the residual energy that is left behind by the many hours of the call-and-response chants I have on replay. Sanskrit is tattooed on my skin, in my bones. When not meditating or chanting, I say "I AM" all day long, in the back of my head. I have learned to quiet my mind, to dispel the voices of the past. I have been learning to send energy out my hands and my heart.

He is a Reiki master. I can already tell he is the lover I have been waiting for.

I can't recall if he said this before or after convincing me to have a drink, but I will never forget his words: "I'm going to teach you about boundaries."

—

He has no car. He has a past. Abused as a child, he hit the streets in his teens where some say he worked as a sex worker and later an "enforcer." Like me, he feels he is in need of forgiveness, but unlike me he feels he has done things that cannot be forgiven.

I introduce him to my spiritual teacher Steve, and it is clear they both feel territorial about me and my unfolding. Months later Steve says, "That man has death all around him." He tells me he can no longer work with me. He cannot be a witness to what is coming next. I should be worried, but instead I am smitten.

—

Lovemaking is just as it was in the dream. Energy pours out of my feet and my toes every time he enters me. This must be that expansion of consciousness everyone around me is seeking.

—

He has had my car for months now. It is hard to explain to people how this happened. I am embarrassed to say that one evening when I could not drive him home, because my son was asleep, he asked to borrow my car. He was to bring it to school the next day, but he tells me it broke down. He has a friend who will fix it, but it will take some time as the man is very busy. A month later I ask where it is parked, so I can get a tow truck and take it to my own mechanic. He will not tell me where it is.

His visits become less frequent. When he does come by, money goes missing. Soon my diamond ring is gone, and my landlord tells me tools are missing from the laundry room/storage space. The landlord says I will have to move.

~

I find a decent apartment in an old house in Kits. It's a two bedroom, and even though it would be nice for Jessie to have his own room, I will have to rent out that second bedroom.

I have graduated from Sprott Shaw with honours and am to be the valedictorian speaker at our graduation ceremony. He has not finished his courses and he owes them money. He still has my car.

I am looking for work and on income assistance. Things continue to go missing. He has weekly garage sales. At one I find my tent, the one that went missing when he helped me move. The one he says he never saw.

~

I am growing tired of his ways. I want my keys back. I want my car.

~

Every visit he brings wine or beer with him. Some days I say, "No, I don't want to drink," but when I do this, he pours me a glass of wine or opens a bottle of beer for me. Sometimes I pour it down the sink. Some days I am not that strong.

One morning, he takes an extra-long shower to remove the haze of his hangover. This seems a good opportunity to take my keys and hide my car. He is not having it. To this day, the fingers he bent back further than they are meant to go still ache when it is damp and cold.

~

I try to leave him many times, but he needs me. He cannot insure a car. He needs mine. Each year when the insurance comes due, I try to decline renewal, but he parks himself at my home until I give in. By now he has raped me and strangled me until I was unconscious. There have been visits from the police. Later I find out police reports make no mention of the rape or the violence. They simply say he was picked up on an outstanding warrant for some other crime.

I am learning the police are no help and that it is better if he is out, if he stays away.

⁓

He can feel me leaving, so I get good at pretending that I am all his. When I do try to leave, he follows me everywhere, even to the grocery store. A remote viewer, he tells me he can see and hear whatever I do. I begin to wonder if this is true. He knows things. One day after I tell a friend that I am considering a move to Winnipeg so I can get rid of him, he calls incessantly until I answer. "You do know that I can find you wherever you go?"

It is becoming increasingly clear that his need for control grows if he suspects I might leave. On occasion he demonstrates his skill as a martial artist, immobilizing me, pushing me against a wall and holding me up, my feet off the ground, his hands on my throat. He reminds me that he can kill me, something my father told my mother many times.

⁓

One day I wake up after a night of heavy drinking. He is gone. My ripped shirt, fat lip, and the blood between my legs are all evidence of his recent presence. I throw out the wine bottles and my shirt. I don't want to look at them or be in that apartment. I take a drive in the wreck of a car that my friend has given me.

I need to think. What can I do?

There is no one to call anymore. No one wants to be on this merry-go-round ride with us. Maybe I should call the police – but I just threw away all the evidence. Besides, the police never do anything.

Maybe it is the alcohol. Having a drink together is how this all began. It is becoming clear that I will never be able to lose this man unless I am sober. Afraid to bring anyone into my life, I become my own sponsor, reminding myself of all I learned the first time in AA. When I do return to AA meetings at six months sober, I only go to meetings at the Longhouse Church, where most of the members are Indigenous. I do this in part because the men there never try to touch me. It angers me to this day that AA was often not a safe space for young women.

Now that I am sober, Dean can sense that he is losing his grip on me. Whenever this happens, he exerts control via physical assault and stalking. He can't break into this home as easily as others in the past. I feel safer, stronger. He becomes more and more desperate. Leaving is a very dangerous time for a woman and yet so many ask, "Why didn't she leave him?" I already knew the answer to this question. My mother had told me often that she knew my dad would kill her if she left. I pray for guidance daily. I know the only way out of this will be if I trust my inner knowingness. I become more watchful, less reactive. I have to do this for my son.

Dean slips up. He becomes so enraged that he hits me in front of my son. Until then he had only hit me when no one was there. I once again call the police. This time, when my five-year-old son shares what he witnessed, the way he had hidden in the bathroom afraid for his life, I can feel that the police officer is truly listening. But I am afraid to trust this until I hear that still-small voice whisper to me, "Tell him everything. This one will do something." My whole body is shaking, my voice wobbles as I say, "This is not the first time that Dean has assaulted me or that I have called the police. It's been happening for years now. No one does anything." He asks me to write a statement, which I do. It is a seven-page handwritten document of what I can remember. Dean is arrested and a no-contact order is put in place.

The crown council who has my case says it is one of the worst he has ever seen. Dean is charged with physical assault. Thanks to the tireless work of many women, domestic violence charges are no longer up to the victim. It is now standard practice that these charges are up to the attending police officer. The rape is not, so it is referred to the sexual assault unit. I am called in for an interview.

The detective from the sexual assault unit has kind eyes, a soft gaze; even so I feel naked knowing what he has no doubt read in the police files. When he says, "If you were my daughter, I would want you to charge him," all I can think is, "Yes, but you are not my father. My father would blame me." Having just completed sixteen weeks of training at Battered Women's Support Services, where I had hopes of working, I know that when it comes to sexual assault of any kind, it is the woman who ends up on trial. A woman with a history like mine doesn't have a chance. I decide not to press charges, a decision that haunts me for years.

We proceed to trial for the domestic violence, and even though the no-contact order is in place, Dean calls often. He follows me, but again when I let the police know, nothing is done. Not only that; his mother gets him a $500-an-hour lawyer. Our mutual friends want to know why I would do this to him. He fails to appear for the first court date.

Every few months he is picked up on an outstanding warrant and signs a promise to appear. A new court date is set and then as each court date passes, he is nowhere to be found. I have to appear at the social services office, as he has reported me for child abuse. I work as a housing coordinator in social housing and have been meeting with child protection workers to set up workshops for tenants whose children are at risk of apprehension. Entering the office, I wonder if I will see anyone I know. Thank Goddess I am sober now or this could go very badly.

Dean still has my car. He is still watching me, but at least I am sober, harder to pin down.

MY BODY A DOORWAY

my body a doorway
between what others say
and all that I can feel

my body a doorway
others have entered
some did not knock
they kicked the door down
until it could no longer close

without boundaries I wandered
between my world and theirs
never fully arriving anywhere

after too many break-ins I installed a steel door
one that no one could enter and then came
the revelation my body is the doorway between dreams
framed flesh filled with longing it needs to breathe

I have two doors now
a screen door
where there is flow of air
but nothing that bites can enter
the other door hard wood
includes a deadbolt
and only I have the key

WHAT TO DO IN AN EMERGENCY

> *The task we must set for ourselves is not to feel secure,*
> *but to be able to tolerate insecurity.*

—ERICH FROMM

The Art of Loving (1956)

1. Call 911.
2. Find a flashlight.
3. Turn off all lights.
4. Enter the bathroom. Lock the door.
5. Wait on the stool in the bathroom.

By the time they get there, he will be gone. The damage will be done.

There will be no witnesses.

His word against yours and yours is never enough. Stay calm or it gets worse. No matter how afraid you are, no matter what he has done

nothing will be done.

CARE(LESS)

my yoni was once a welcoming place
but now resists entry
once a place of passion   of abandon
now a petulant place   one of refusal
she says she has done enough
that you were reckless with her

THE LAST DROP

you were my bottom
the coffee grounds in my cup
bitter and dark
you stained everything

like all bad habits
you kept returning
the penny I could not throw away
no matter how hard I tried to leave
you always found me

you were my bottom
the coffee grounds in my cup
bitter and dark
you stained everything

MAKING ROOM

daytime dropping down
becoming   moving across
breasts full
   I scan my body search
tissue and bone memories of you
I am learning to exorcise
what you left behind

at night thin-skinned thoughts
of you leave me sleepless
not all who haunt us are dead

I may never fully remove you
from my body   my memory

                                        but I can
                                        use mantras
                                        to push you
                                        to the side

where you will remain

Belonging:
Breaking the Curse

There are spirit voices talking, weaving threads of
disparate stories into one great aural tapestry of talk
that will outlast us all – the story of a place called
Kanata that has come to mean "our home."

—RICHARD WAGAMESE

Runaway Dreams (2011)

He Who Welcomed Me, an Ojibwe artist I met in AA, keeps
telling me that I belong, and not just in AA. He hands me a copy
of Richard Wagamese's *Keeper'n Me*. He tells me I will see myself
in many of the pages. I do.

He Who Welcomed Me lives in Native Housing. My son Jessie
and I visit him often, and whenever we drop by, he shares
teachings with us as he carves or paints. If painting, he shows us
how he practises over and over to get those very fine lines, most
with gentle curves. He tells us that he is experimenting with
traditional West Coast red and black but bringing in "the softer
Ojibwe ways." Telus has commissioned a piece from him. At my
one-year cake, he gifts me with one of the prints, 20/80. It still
hangs in my living room, a reminder of all that we learned from
He Who Welcomed Me.

Sobriety the second time round is even harder than the first.
The first time it was 1986, I was thirty-three, attractive, and single.
There was always someone who was willing to keep me company
if I needed it. There were sober dances and after every meeting
carloads of us would head to some coffee shop. I sponsored
people, took them to meetings, was available for phone calls night
and day. I helped some through the Twelve Steps. I had been
taught to pay it forward and did this so much that they used to call
my car "the God Mobile." I never had to spend much time alone.
I only had myself to care for.

After moving to Vancouver, I went into therapy and saw a psychologist every week. My regular salary barely covered my living expenses, which meant I had to work one extra shift each week. Eight hours of work for one hour of her time. It was hard, but that was nothing compared to life as a newly sober, low-income, single mom living in social housing and coming out of an abusive relationship. Not only was it hard to get to meetings, but I was traumatized and had lost my place in AA. All of my closest AA friends now had ten or more years of sobriety. I was neither an old-timer nor a newcomer. I had all the AA teachings in my head and because Dean was still stalking me, I was afraid to bring anyone into my life. I largely kept to myself and only felt safe at Native meetings, as we called them in those days.

My son was struggling in school and had been diagnosed with ADHD, which I now wonder about. Was it ADHD or was he just traumatized by the violence he had witnessed, by having a low-income single mom?

It was hard to get my feet under me, especially since Dean was ever present in my mind and would do things like turn up on my first day at Liberty Thrift store, where I had just been hired to help manage the store and bring in more donations for battered women escaping abusive relationships. It was a lot, and for a time I considered sending my son to live with my brother and his wife in Winnipeg. I just needed one year to get my feet under me. My brother registered Jessie in the evangelical Christian school that his sister-in-law worked at, but in the end I couldn't let my son go. I couldn't bear the feelings that came with thinking of a life without him and did worry that I might not get him back.

Sometimes it is hard to know what is best for a child. As parents we are faced with so many difficult decisions, but after many tears I decided he was my son, my responsibility, and we belonged together.

That summer my brother took him for three weeks, and when Jessie returned he had photos of all the things he had done. Time spent at a cabin at Lake of the Woods and a trip down to North Dakota. Each photo made me ache inside. He was so thin, seemed so frail, and had an empty look in his eyes. I had to do better. He needed me. I had to stay sober. I owed him that much and more.

Eventually, we moved to a housing co-operative where I had bars on my windows and my apartment faced a busy courtyard. I felt safe there.

I needed a job. After all that happened with my stalker boyfriend, my manager had suggested I take a medical leave, and since my job there was a contract that meant my contract was over.

I had already lost another job and moved several times, each time hoping to hide from Dean, but he would always find me. Once he showed up while I was in the middle of moving. He stayed to help me, winking and smiling at me the whole time while inside all I felt was fear creeping further into my body.

I was forty-one, desperately trying to hold onto my dignity while once again losing a job, a good job, because a man has had his hands on me.

~

Most days feel impossible. I am tired. I now understand why my mom always said she was so tired. But at least I am sober.

~

On particularly bad days, the days when I don't know what to do with myself, Jessie and I visit He Who Welcomed Me. One day Jessie comments on a picture that He Who Welcomed Me had just finished. It was an all-seeing eagle with piercing eyes that followed you around the room. There was life in the drawing. Jessie felt the power in it.

"If you like it, I will give it to you. That is our way."

To a seven-year-old who has known poverty, this seems extraordinary. I know my son and that he will want to test the truth of this, so am not surprised when he lifts his hand, points to the picture of the wolf hanging on the wall.

Now I am uncomfortable. I know that He Who Welcomed Me makes his living selling his art and often has trouble finding the money for art supplies.

I say nothing. Words don't work with Jessie. Instead, I move towards my son, lift my right hand. Soft touch is a gentler way of asking him to pause, to reflect on what he does next, but He Who Welcomed Me intercepts my hand. Soon Jessie is the recipient of another drawing, one of a burial ground. Those three art pieces travelled with us from home to home through many years.

Each carried a message.

The eagle spoke to us of love, of being close to the Creator and able to see far. There is power in seeing.

The wolf reminded us to be humble, that we needed others. Being part of a pack teaches us to be right sized, that we are part of a whole. We need to know our place. Hold others up.

The four poles of the burial scaffolding held bodies wrapped in birch bark. Ancestors raised to the sky. Red cloth flapping in the wind.

This one took the longest to reveal itself to me. I knew that even though I love graveyards, I did not want to be buried. It did not feel right to me. There is dignity in being held up.

I would later learn it was so much more than that. Some teachings take time.

It is many years later, when my father dies, that I understand the burial ground picture was intended to open my mind about just how differently my Indigenous brothers and sisters view death. Raised Anglican, all I had known was funerals and graveyards filled with flowers, plaques in chapels. Sanitized events.

My baby brother is an evangelical Christian and, since Dad had no spiritual practices that we know of, my brother decides to have Dad's service at his church. The main room is one of those chapels the size of a football field. We don't have that many attending, so rent one of the smaller rooms.

As I sit in that room full of people, many of whom I don't know, all I can think is, "Is this what Dad would have wanted?" I realize that I have no idea what he believes. He never said, and I never asked.

Once I'm home, the mother of an Anishinaabe friend passes away. From her I learn all that she and her family did to support their loved one in making the change of worlds. Things like keeping a fire for four days while their loved one revisited everywhere they had been. Suddenly all those visits from the dead made sense. Not knowing the teachings, I had noticed that the recently deceased would drop by, and because I could hear them, they would sometimes leave me messages to pass on to others they loved but who could not hear.

I learn about the need for spirit food and think our ghosts must be very hungry. We had never offered food to our dead.

~

Later I learn from Dr. Malidoma Somé about the Dagara's teachings about death. They, like many Indigenous people, nurture the relationship between the living and the dead. Since losing my first brother, I knew the veil was thin but had no one to talk to about this or to show me how to grieve. Given this I listened intently as Malidoma spoke about the "shrieking guttural wail" of the women announcing a death, asking the village to prepare for the grief ritual. He says, "Mourners should never be left alone," and I think how alone I was every time someone in my family died. It is not my place to share more of his teachings. They are in his book, *Ritual: Power, Healing and Community*. They are his alone to share.

What he shared helped me to see why it took so long for me to mourn. We need ritual and yes, for some that is a funeral, but that was not enough for me. I needed to be embraced, to be held by a community that understood that death is a part of life. I needed ritual and a community that understood that death is not the end, nor was heaven the goal for some of us.

I did know that the dead were still with me. They talked to me often, but much of what they expressed was regret.

Without the rituals and Ceremony of my Indigenous Ancestors, I had wrong ideas about the dead. They had been trying to tell me something I could not hear. I had no frame of reference for it all. But they never relented, gently gesturing towards people and experiences that would bring me the teachings I needed.

~

One day I find a notice board that has a small hand-written note from Richard Wagamese and his partner Debra Powell. I can't believe my eyes. I have just finished reading *Keeper'n Me* and feel a deep connection to Richard and his story. The notice is an invitation to join him and Debra at the Longhouse Church for a Native Talking Circle. I call to register.

That night I dream of Richard. We are in the Longhouse Church. He is at the front of the church, and I am at the door. He speaks to me with his mind, his voice like a child crying out for his mother.

When I attend my first circle, Richard is standing in the doorway of the Longhouse Church. He looks and feels exactly as he did in my dream.

It is a sign. I am sure of this.

We take our seats. It is all couples, and there is one empty seat in the circle. It is next to me. Acutely aware that I am alone, I see the deep love that Richard and Debra have for one another. I want what they have. But who would want me now?

I begin to pray.

We meet monthly and eventually move the circle to Richard and Debra's living room, which is much cozier than the large and hollow-feeling wooden church.

Every time Richard smudges us, he ends by touching the top of our heads with his broad eagle-feather fan. Each time he does this, I have to steady myself as the power of the eagle feather, the Medicines, and his kind attention makes its way through my weary mind and body.

At every circle Richard shares a teaching from his Elders. He often speaks about his life as a writer and about *Ragged Company*, the book he is currently working on. When he shares, I feel the gentle flutter of a hummingbird's wings inside me, reminding me I have gifts.

I begin to dream of being a writer and remember what my astrologer friend, She Who Saved Me, the one from Maple Ridge

Treatment Centre, had said about my being a writer later in life. Once again I had thought she was wrong. But was she?

———

I think often about the dream I had the night before our first circle. In it I am standing in the doorway of the church aware that I am crossing a threshold into a whole new world. Having been raised in a family that denied their Indigenous ancestry had left me feeling on the outside of.everything. Standing in a doorway is a great metaphor for the way I have lived, but it did not come from me.

I once heard Fred Wah say it on a podcast when describing life as one who was biracial. He felt like he had stood in the doorway of two rooms all his life and that he could see into both rooms, so knew both worlds. Although I can appreciate the truth of this for him, I feel differently about being biracial.

It is true I do tend to stand in the doorway, but not knowing the languages or cultures of my Icelandic and Métis Ancestors left me feeling as if I do not know either world. For me, "standing in the doorway" speaks to the fact that as a person of between who sought out other persons of between, I have stood in the doorways of many worlds. Never sure of my place and suspicious of the need to always agree, I never fully entered any room. I always kept a part of myself outside and did not feel like I belonged anywhere.

It was my Ojibwe brothers Richard and He Who Saved Me that helped me begin to feel as if I belonged in the Indigenous world. Sharon Jinkerson-Brass, a Saulteaux Elder (the Saulteaux are a branch of the Ojibwe People) and dear friend, took me a step further. She told me that the Ojibwe were known as the "Hummingbird People," because we could hold a hummingbird in our hands. This vision carries me. My gentle spirit is soothed by this image. Sharon always makes me feel like I belong, that it is okay to have a gentler nature.

Sharon also told me that as Indigenous women we need to know who we are and who we come from, and until we do we are vulnerable. I do have Anishinaabe Ancestors, including those who were what we once called Ojibwe. Sharon, Richard, and He Who

Saved Me did at one time all say that they were Ojibwe, a term I have seen in my genealogy searches. Many who are Indigenous do have Ancestors from a number of Nations. The way we were named in the past was Anglicized versions of our Nations, but many are reclaiming the names they once used. The shifting terms have made it hard to know exactly who I come from, but thankfully I can lean into my Métis Ancestors comfortably, as they are well documented. Adding to this, Sharon has claimed me and reminds me regularly who I am.

WHO OWNS THIS LAND?

renters remain   unwelcome
dislodged by inequality
pushed from one home   to the next
they bring their potted plants
find a place for them on the new patio
until they can't afford a patio
and still no honest answer
to who owns this Land

I know it must be hard to feel
sorry for renters like me
who could once afford a balcony
when this was once a forest
before my Métis Ancestor
brought those who came with HBC blankets

I know who owns this Land   and it is not me

        yet here I am with nowhere to go

            forever trapped in rentals

a little too familiar with basement suites
where no sharing of the yard shall take place
and when their mother-in-law needs the suite

we will have to move   again!

ASKING FOR A FRIEND

how many intersections must
I have before my feelings matter
I can give you the list   it is long
as is my life   at sixty-five I am
a boomer who has
boomeranged back to the bottom
over and over again

those damn intersections kept coming for me
wrong colour but not wrong enough
low income but not low enough for some
disabled but invisibly so again not enough
no degrees but well-read is never enough
a renter familiar with co-op living
I am in need of four-way stop signs and
a traffic cop to sort out all these intersections

FRASER RIVER FORGETTING

around New West we find many mentions of Simon
the one the river is now named after
his Métis interpreter and guide forgotten

there are no statues   no plaques devoted to
my great-great-great-grandfather, Waccan
a.k.a. Jean-Baptiste Boucher
a voyageur who spoke many languages
and is said to be the most famous
Métis man this side of the Rockies
he remains unnamed in most history books
there are no statues   no plaques devoted to
his place in the *settling* of these lands

now buried at Fort St. James
I think I just felt him roll over
did he know what he was bringing?

some say his wife, my Tse'khene great-great-great-grandmother
Nancy McDougall helped save Sir James Douglas
from Chief Kw'eh's knife
she too was erased while her Scottish father
can be found in many historical accounts

as I sit by the river I am here to ask
if this erasure is a silent blessing
I am here to ask if it is ever good to forget
to ask for forgiveness from the Coast Salish

it is their place names that matter most
forgotten by some but never gone
it is their Ancestors that sit with me

      by this river, the Stó:lō

now commonly called the Fraser

             a place of forgetting for so many

ERASURE

dedicated to my great-great-great-grandfather Osh-pih-kah-kahn

a.k.a. Louis Godon III (1836–1912)

tales told to census takers include
name changes
Osh-pih-kah-kahn
becomes Louis Godon
in five short years
my great-great-great-grandfather's
census records go from
"Native, Catholic, 1 married man"
                   to "Catholic, 1 married man"
his Métis wife unnamed
listed as "1 married woman"
did my grandfather know
that our Indigenous roots
would lead to me?
a granddaughter born
over one hundred years later
did he know his granddaughter
would look back, collect him and
all the other "half breeds" into her arms
having known the pain
of being unacceptably impure
when really all we are is

"the result of the love of thousands"

when we talk of race

of the intermingling

why is it that we never

talk about the love

that brought some of us together

CENSUS DATA

Louis Godon was born *circa* 1836 at St. Agathe, the son of Louise Godon II and Elizabeth Isaac. He was born at the Red River Settlement in 1836 where his family had moved after the closure of the Pembina Mission in 1821. His family appears in the Red River Census for the years 1838, 1840, and 1843.

GODON, Louis

#214, Louis Godon, age __, Native, Catholic, 1 married man, 1 married woman, 1 son (-16), 3 total inhabitants, 1 house, 1 stable, 2 mares, 1 ox, 1 bull, 2 cows, 3 calves, 4 pigs, 1 cart, 2 acres. (1838 E.5/9)

#229, Louis Godon, age __, Native, Catholic, 1 married man, 1 married woman, 2 sons (-16), 4 total inhabitants, 1 house, 1 stable, 1 horse, 1 mare, 3 oxen, 1 bull, 2 carts, 2 acres. (1840 E.5/10)

#207, Louis Godin, age __, Rupert's Land, Catholic, 1 married man, 1 married woman, 2 sons (-16), 1 daughter (+15), 1 daughter (-15), 6 total inhabitants, 1 house, 1 stable, 1 horse, 2 mares, 2 oxen, 1 pig, 2 carts, 1 canoe, 2 acres. (1843 E.5/11)

HIDDEN

she was in possession
of a gift that required no references
her story a weapon made of words
serpentine it slivered between legs
around chairs under coffee tables
someone once found it
lying upon the bookshelf
its companions absent
there were demands for an explanation

she was not Christian
said her prayers to the Ancestors
and with her sister she braided sweetgrass
all things passed from one to the other

she kept her eyes fixed upon a map
that no one else can see
she rapidly repeats the names
of every lake and river
she follows her own path
will not say where she is going

OLD AND WISE

soon to be sky-bound the stars await
until then I long to be all that I am
to move between day and night

a cloud   floating

　　my fingers filling with sunlight

my limbs beaming brightness

　　　my hair radiant   silvery wisps

　　　　shining in the moonlight

my body buoyant and blameless

I long to lie low   stay close to the earth
until the wandering wind persuades movement

and in the morning   full luminous
I will be bright breezy

my arms   my legs
feathery wisps of innocence

no fingers pointing   mine now tender tendrils

　　　　gesturing towards

　　　　　the earth

old and wise I will have stories to tell

WHERE IS HOME?

this body carried many children
only one made it out alive
rejections in the form of miscarriages
followed by decisions to abort
left me the birth mother of one
my body – sinew and bone
I can no longer feel

looking back, I believe it happened over time
buried under laundry, the to-do list
and all the jobs I hated
my body planned her departure
as my spirit wandered the hallways of the past
tethered to pain I thought we could ignore

I tried *positive thinking*
bought Post-it Notes for all the
JUST MOVE ON messages on mirrors
computer monitors a place for self-praise
for all the "I'm very, very good at my job" lies
until my skin reads like a map to nowhere

twenty years later here I am
still running
running out of time
I ask my body to come back
into my awareness
I make promises to care for her
while I worry I will not
not because I don't want to
but because my spirit
is already on the move

    leading my body – sinew and bone – home

Blended:
A Family Constructed,
Then Deconstructed

It is said that in every loss there is an opportunity to uncover and heal the losses of a lifetime.

—STEPHEN LEVINE

Unattended Sorrow: Recovering from Loss and Reviving the Heart (2005)

On Jessie's fourteenth birthday, we move in with Garry, my third and hopefully final husband. He insists we live in Point Grey, a place where Garry has lived for the past thirteen years.

I am not comfortable here. When I go into the local shops, the staff often ask me things like, "Are you working in the area?" As a biracial woman whose skin darkens when exposed to the sun, I look more like the nannies and the housekeepers than the homeowners who employ them. But it is more than that. I have that head-down walk those of us who have not had privilege sometimes get.

Jessie will once again have to change schools. As a child, I hated all the moving. Each time I would have to figure out the territorial landscape of each school.

I don't want my son to go to the local secondary school, Lord Byng. Many who attend that school are wealthy and Jessie is the child of a low-income single mother. All he has known are basement suites, social housing, and co-op housing. We are renters and I know how some of the rich feel about renters. Not only that – Jessie is in grade ten and coming from Killarney Secondary School. It's a big leap in terms of class. As I contemplate this, I remember that when my son was three, I had had a vivid vision of him attending Kitsilano Secondary School, so that is my first call. I beg the principal at Kits to accept him as a cross-boundary student. Fortunately for us, the principal was once at Killarney and knows us both, as I was an engaged parent. Even so, it takes some convincing but, in the end, he agrees to accept Jessie.

Our new apartment is one of the most luxurious homes I have ever had. It is also a hotbed of paranormal activity. At night there are visitations. One man keeps getting into bed with me. I can feel he is lonely and confused. I can tell that he is looking for his wife as he spoons me. Every night I have to tell him to go, that I am not his wife. He is harmless.

In my experience most ghosts are harmless. They are just lost souls seeking connection. They do take direction. You can ask them to leave knowing they are forgetful and may return again and again.

There are others. One is scary. He stands at the end of the bed and presses on the mattress to taunt me. The still, quiet voice in my head always says, "Don't look. Never look at him." Every time he presents himself, demanding my attention, I don't look, and eventually he goes away. I wonder if this place is so active because there is a very large electrical box right outside the kitchen window. I am afraid to tell my husband about all this – he will think I'm losing my grip on reality.

One day in the hallway, I stop to give my husband a hug. I smell death on him. We have just started living together and not only can I smell cancer, but it is deadly. For weeks I struggle with whether or not to tell him.

We get a call from Garry's sister-in-law, Kathy. She says that his brother, Ken, has lung cancer, and he does not have long. Whoosh … I feel him. I see now that it was Ken that I had sensed in the hallway, through Garry. Ken is a man I have never met, but he has a similar energy signature to my hubby. He is afraid and has been hanging around his little brother.

I can feel he needs someone to be with him, to listen. Garry tells me that his brother was into things like sex magic and Aleister Crowley. I can tell that he is worried that he may have brought negative forces into his life. He is afraid about where he might be going. I don't believe in hell. I reassure him.

A few days later, in the wee hours of the morning, I feel him leave. The next morning we get the call; he has passed.

～

Garry heads to Prince George to help his sister-in-law Kathy and his nephew Jaime with funeral arrangements. I do not go. I have never met these people, but I do know the pain of loss.

～

Kathy has never been without Ken. She is not well, has never been well. He has taken care of many things over the years. All the things that she cannot. We all wonder how she will manage.

～

We get a call. Kathy is being flown to Vancouver. The hospital in Prince George is not equipped to deal with her illness.

Her son Jaime will be alone.

He is fourteen and living in the country outside of Prince George. Everyone decides he should stay there and continue going to school. The neighbours and his friend's parents will help. He and I begin conversing regularly on MSN Messenger. I soon learn he has a sense of humour and that he is fiercely independent. He is in love.

～

The first time I meet Jaime he has come to visit his mom at Vancouver General Hospital. He gets off the plane, a string bean of a boy with long, greasy red hair he has cut himself. He has no bags and is wearing dirty clothes. Even so I can see he is a handsome lad. He is just six months older than my son. They are nothing alike: Jaime is a gamer, a Dungeons & Dragons master, and Jessie is a skateboarding, pot-smoking teen.

～

Jaime is alone for months. We communicate regularly on MSN Messenger. His mother is not going to recover. A will is drawn up. Garry and I are named as backup guardians.

Jessie and I drive up to Prince George to make sure Jaime has everything he needs. His house is like the houses you see on those TV shows about hoarders. I have never been in a home like this one. There are cobwebs everywhere. It smells bad. I am concerned for Jaime, but to him this is all very normal. He says he is okay. I don't agree, but I am new to the Ward family and don't feel I have much of a say. Besides, he is in love. That is all that matters to him.

———

I take Jaime shopping to buy his mother a nice nightgown for her cremation. He feels she would want that. No one plans to be present when her body is cremated. I go and sit in the chapel, a sacred witness to the burning of her body. No one else is there. At least she has a nice nightgown on.

———

Everyone is talking about what to do with Jaime. There is talk of him living in Chilliwack with Garry's brother, who already has twelve children at home. Five are his biological children and the others are Stó:lō Nation children, some adopted and some fostered. I just can't see Jaime, the goth gamer, living in the bible belt with so many people after having been the only child for much of his fourteen years on the planet. He does have an adopted brother, Jake, who is much older, but they've fallen out of touch.

I tell Garry, "We need to take him." Everyone agrees, but Jaime resists. He does not want to come with us.

He is in love.

The drive home with him, a teenager who has lost both parents and is leaving his love, his whole life, behind is long. He is angry. We make promises we hope we can keep. She can come visit. He can go there. The time will pass quickly. Of course it doesn't.

———

I am now mother to two teenage boys, both fourteen. I am once again sitting in the principal's office at Kits begging them to take a child who is out of their territory. They agree. Jaime will begin school at Kits.

I take him shopping for clothes. He likes black, and most of his selections reflect this preference. I take him to my hairdresser, who gives him a cool haircut. We all agree she should dye his hair black. She suggests a red streak. His first day at school he glides in, handsome, in black with that red streak, but not before sitting wordless in the car with Jessie and me. Both of us can feel he needs time to take everything in. We sit with him, careful not to interrupt the silence he needs. Once he's ready, Jessie walks him to the office.

⌒

Jaime and I are a matched set. Both of us broken early in life, both creative. He is an artist. I am a writer. I have always gravitated towards those with strong spirits, spirits seasoned by trauma and loss.

⌒

He has never been to the dentist and rarely, if ever, to a doctor. He is six-foot-three and one hundred and ten pounds. He eats rice one grain at a time. He drinks Coke all day long and will only eat white bread. Jessie and I are *health nuts*, we never have things like Coke or white bread in our home.

I take Jaime to the doctor, who is horrified by the fact that he has a deformed chest. Now all those baggy T-shirts make sense. He has been hiding this. The doctor says, "How do both lungs fit in there?" X-rays and blood work are ordered.

Jaime understandably has a fear of doctors and hospitals. His father and his mother both went to the hospital one day and never returned. He nearly faints when they take his blood, and he has to be medicated when getting dental work. Thankfully, his small cage-like chest does not appear to be affecting his health.

The momma bear in me is strong. I hold his hand whenever he lets me. He needs me, but he resents this need.

⌒

We had many good years together. He graduated from Kits with honours and went to the Arts Institute. His career as a graphic artist was just taking off when he was diagnosed with a rare and aggressive form of cancer.

I had always been afraid that I would suffer the same fate as my mother, that I would lose a child. Now it was happening.

THE BEREAVED

magnetic images expose peril
become a diagnosis   become sorrow
unattended our needs inescapable
they avalanche down our backs
until we turn to the web
how many will offer condolences?
comment on web walls of wailing
tap   tap   tap   thoughts

through fingers of longing
we pull on hearts
strung too tight   the cords
between us a hunger
insatiable   it feasts on sadness
as our regrets ruminate
we find ourselves alone

with fingers on keys   we know that
feelings cannot make their way across the web
but some empaths and poets find ways
to make the distance shorter
while others offer to teach us
how to meditate
to become fortunate via podcasts

companions in pleasure we seek
to display ourselves in this "mirage of tenderness"
we ponder the velocity of words
the way they travel between us
forgetting that we are the doorway
we are this place of tension   of unattended sorrow
lost in the economy of language

there is a cost not discussed
it remains hidden in the
fine print of online relationships

DEAR NEPHEW

a raven flew into your birdcage chest
having grown silently large
it pressed against

esophagus   crushing

      vocal cords

insistent it pushed

your heart   unrelenting
in the crowding of a lung
that no one can find

my sweet boy you are death's companion
first your father and his lungs
then your mother and your old life
now you

I think of all the years you meant to live
the way you held us in hope and said
you were 100% committed to staying

I knew it would take more than we had
that your body would become the scene of a crime
where we would find ourselves

unwilling
witnesses
with paperwork
on our fridge

DO NOT RESUSCITATE

in bold letters

we became accomplices in a reality
that said there was no one to call
one where the sunflowers have the face
of your friend and a woman wearing
a purple coat   a leopard tam
sits reading a newspaper

you said she never speaks

her interruptions heard as pages turning
even so   it was hard for you to follow TV shows

you wanted a storyboard
a map of the merging so you could follow along

in this liminal space we share   I sit
in a chair beside you   thinking I should get up
sort that bookcase but

tired from trail of care I pass thought to you
and you say you see me in the corner

when I ask
what am I doing
you say
          looking
at the bookcase

you said that I am always looking
at the bookcase   perhaps I was hoping

       for another ending

now even the unfinished
box of Raisin Bran
leads me back to you

your bread-crumb trail of things
cellphones   laptops
artwork   lamps

what to do with wallets
their contents worn
all things we must now find
something to do with
when what we really want is you

       we are left

with questions   so ask

    did we do enough

the response is always the same
I hear the raven flutter his wings
he has you now   he wants you to fly

Finding Love:
Two Birds on a Wire

There is no such thing as two people – whether baby and mother, two lovers, or teacher and student – being perfectly in sync with each other's needs and wishes. Real intimacy arises from an ongoing process of connection that at some point is disrupted and then, ideally, repaired.

—PILAR JENNINGS
"Looking into the Eyes of a Master" (2014)

When I lived in Winnipeg, my best friend Laurie and I would often visit the Chocolate Shop on Portage Avenue, a place well known for their tea-leaf readers and psychics. I was twenty-one when a gifted reader told me that I will know love, that we will be like two birds sitting on a wire. I could feel what she meant. This would be a gentle love, the kind that is rare. I spend the next twenty-nine years looking for him, and at times I think she must have been wrong. But then I would remember how I felt as she spoke. It had to be real.

⁓

After my relapse in 1993, I rebuilt my life, had a new career, and was ready to date again when I finally found him at a New Year's Eve sober dance. My friend had saved a chair for me, and as I sit down, I hear myself announce, "I am going to find the man of my dreams tonight." I'm surprised by my own words but soon understand.

Our table is a place of coming and going. Only one chair remains unoccupied. Garry arrives and fills that empty spot.

He is what some call a cool drink of water, a jazz man, who moves with a grace that is uncommon for someone his size. We begin to talk, and when the seat next to me opens up he moves closer. I can feel his knee near mine. I try to ignore this as we explore the usual *what do you do* banter. I find out he is a consultant for the federal government. He develops and teaches courses.

I have been dreaming of becoming a consultant, of being self-employed. I tell him about my business plan, a "bring your soul to work" consulting company, that I have been studying mediation and facilitation for years now.

My skin is tingling, but I am afraid to trust this feeling. I met him once before at a board meeting. A mutual friend invited us both to the meeting, and she's been talking to me about him. She has a crush, she says that he is married but unhappy. She is waiting for him to leave his wife. She will be there when he needs her.

Remembering this, I say I need to go for a walk. I need a moment. He asks to join me. I reluctantly agree.

~

On our walk he pulls out a cigarette. Ordinarily I hate cigarette smoke and have a strict rule. I never date smokers. Yet I barely notice the smoke.

He walks close to me. My skin is once again tingling but – another rule – I don't date married men. I feel irritated with him, with myself. I ask, "Aren't you married?" He says, "No, I have left my wife. I have a new apartment. Just a small studio suite."

A few years sober and he has left his wife. So many people do this. The poor person who put up with our alcoholic antics sometimes doesn't get to reap the benefits of a sober partner. Too often once "recovered" we just move on. I feel sorry for his ex, but I am excited by the fact that he is available.

~

The next day I call my friend, the one who had a crush on him. I need to ask just how serious this crush is. She does have a few crushes. In fact, it might be hard to find a boyfriend given the number of men she has dibs on.

I ask for permission to pursue him. She says, "Sure!"

~

Our first date is on my fiftieth birthday. Hoping to see him again, I throw myself a birthday party and invite Garry.

The day after the party I tell my friend, "I'm going to marry that man."

I wish I could tell you things got easier once Garry came along. Promises of marriage are not promises of ease. "For better or for worse" is in the marriage vows for a reason. There was a brief honeymoon period. Hot sex in his studio apartment, a place where we sat on the floor and talked for hours at a time.

Sitting with him cross-legged on the floor, I learn he is not like all the other AA guys I have been dating for years now. He has had privilege. He was married for twenty-six years, has a five-bedroom, four-bathroom home with a movie room and three wood-burning fireplaces in Point Grey. His son and ex-wife live in this home filled with expensive artwork and antiques. I live in a two-bedroom apartment in a co-op. Any new furniture I have was purchased on a payment plan at the Brick. My artwork is posters or prints that I have attached to the walls with thumb tacks, as I can't afford to frame them.

Many women would be excited at having found a man of means, but I was not. Always aware of power imbalances, the differences frightened me.

Early on in our conversations, we nearly break up while discussing civil disobedience. I tell him my son and I protested against Premier Gordon Campbell's policies, that one time a group of us joined the Anti-Poverty Committee, walked from Trimble Park to Gordon Campbell's home. As I speak, Garry's face gets redder and redder. Now grey-haired, this former redhead can turn shades of red I have never seen before; he sputters, "I lived down the street from Gordon. My wife and his were friends. I worked on his campaign."

He feels it is never right to go to someone's home like that. I try to explain that our homes were under threat, as the premier's attempt to balance the budget included cutting much-needed funding for low-income housing and other subsidies. I tell Garry that once some people entered the premier's yard, I decided to leave the protest, as that felt too invasive, but that I stood by the need to take the discussion to his "safe" neighbourhood. I don't recall how the conversation ended, but I do know that this was the beginning of many discussions about the differences in our lives.

⁓

I am happy to leave co-op life behind. All that committee work has been exhausting. I am not happy about being in Point Grey, but I do love our apartment. I have never lived in a home like this one. It is spacious, the windows and hardwood floors go on forever. Our bedroom is as large as any living room I have ever had, but more importantly, the energy in the place is off the charts. This apartment is an active place, filled with spirits. My intuition is on high alert.

As we unpack, I begin to set up altars in various locations throughout our new home. Garry says, "Those things belong in the bedroom." He tells me that I can only have altars in the bedroom. I agree but not fully. When he is not looking, I sit a Buddha on the dining room table. A few days later Quan Yin appears in the kitchen. Over time, more and more altar items make their way into the living room. Soon there is a round table with a black scarf for a table cloth, it is a Medicine Wheel altar. We are in need of balance.

As many will know, sacred items direct us. They tell me where they want to be, and I always listen. He will just have to get used to it.

⁓

Living with Garry is not easy. Our differences keep biting us in the ass.

His ex-wife often acts as if he is still her husband. There is always something at the house that needs attention. The hot tub is not working, a light bulb needs changing, or she has things she needs him to take to the Sally Ann. I do my best to be supportive. I am now an Enforcement Officer with the BC Family Maintenance Program, where I enforce child support and spousal support. Ninety-five percent of payors are men. I hear stories daily about how so many of these men get new girlfriends or wives and how his new partner expects him to devote all his time and money to her children.

I don't want to be that woman.

Many days I worry that I have made the wrong decision. Giving up my housing security – a two-bedroom apartment in a co-op that has subsidy whenever you need it – is a big thing to lose. Soon I am on a medical leave from work, as the pain from fibromyalgia has made it impossible for me to sit at a computer for eight and a half hours a day. Between the shift at work and the long drive from Alma and Tenth to the office in Burnaby, it is all too much.

Why did I agree to live so far from where I work? I know it is because I wanted him. I wanted him the second he sat down at my table on New Year's Eve. I still want him, fifteen years later.

It is not easy being with a man who has two ex-partners, each with a child. I have no real ex; Jessie's father has never wanted to claim him. My life is uncomplicated. Garry's is not. The push-pull of these women and his guilt about abandoning his children leave him numb. Even so, we manage to be a family. The Kirtons and the Wards. Once Jaime joins us, there are two of each.

We have to move. Now that we have Jaime, we need a third bedroom. A fourth would be nice. I am a writer now, a stay-at-home mom, dreaming of the kind of home you can raise teenagers in. As the tension between Garry and me grew, the tightness in my body worsened. There are times I wonder if this relationship is the cause of my body's downfall.

He is not abusive in the ways my father was. He never says unkind things. On the other hand, he doesn't say much of anything, and at times he is utterly absent, unreachable. I am essentially a single parent of two teenage boys, one of whom was orphaned and is suffering in ways that bring back memories of my brothers dying. I want to leave, but I want a family more. I love being the mom of these two boys. I love our family dinners, the feel of a real home.

So much has happened since Garry and I first met.

I have learned to follow my life coach's advice. Observing that I was good at leaving and not good at staying, he suggested I learn to "lean into the relationship" whenever I feel like leaving. Between that teaching and the one that says, "We should see each other new every day," I have managed to not only stay but to be a sacred witness to my husband's unfolding. Together we have built a life based on the spiritual teachings found in AA and the understanding that all we can expect from one another is *progress not perfection*. Garry's path that of a mystical scientist, ever curious about life. I am more eclectic, and my path deeply connected to the divine feminine, to the land and the body. We never try to convert one another, but talk often about what we are learning. We both feel seen and heard and when things get hard, we have a common language, the teachings of AA.

I now know what love is.

⁓

Our time together has included walking our nephew Jaime home when, at twenty-four, he was diagnosed with a rare and aggressive form of cancer. By then he had his own apartment and a girlfriend who was just as much into gaming as he was. Both of them were animators; they had met while students at the Art Institute of Vancouver. He had just been told that someone from DreamWorks Animation had commented on some of the work he had done for *The Mr. Peabody & Sherman Show* while working at DHX Media. It all crumbled in one instant. He spent the next few months at the BC Cancer Agency receiving treatments. The doctors were *cautiously optimistic.* By then Garry and I were in bankruptcy, living in a small one-bedroom apartment in a building where Garry was the resident manager.

Once Jaime was back home, we tried to support him from across town but it was hard. Between Garry's workload, my chronic pain, and the continual worry about money, both Garry and I were exhausted. We often felt that we were letting him down and did try to convince him and his girlfriend to move to our building when an apartment opened up.

But Jaime was determined to live independently, so we said little, did what we could, until one day after his girlfriend had left him and his roommate was out of town for a week, Jaime called to say he was hungry, too weak to prepare food, and he wanted me to come make him dinner. When I arrived, I could see he was too frail to care for himself and suggested he come home with me. He agreed but wouldn't even pack a bag, as it was just going to be one night. I knew death was near and all that mattered now was that he go at his own pace. He was not ready to admit defeat. I did not argue. His one night became two months. Soon there was a hospital bed in our living room. This time Garry was engaged, and caring for Jaime transformed us both.

I fell even more in love with Garry as I witnessed the way he attended to his nephew's needs.

When the care aides would offer to lift Jaime's frail body onto the portable toilet, Jaime would say, "No. Garry can do it." The child who trusted no one, who came to us not once but twice dirty, alone, and afraid, felt safe in Garry's strong arms. For two long months, we took turns caring for Jaime. I had the graveyard shift, as Garry had to work during the day. He didn't start work until 9 a.m. and was in and out of the suite all day, which meant I could sleep in the morning.

In the evening we all watched *Dancing with the Stars*. That year, Drew from *Property Brothers* was one of the celebrities. Jaime was a fan of his, so he was happy to watch the show. After each dance, we would all try to guess what score the contestants would get.

Once Garry went to bed, Jaime and I would watch *Four Weddings*. Again, we had fun guessing who would get the highest scores. There was always a lot of laughter.

⸻

The day before Jaime died, he nearly left us. His body evacuated everything. We made frantic calls to his home-care nurse, who was in our apartment within what seemed like minutes. She took his pulse and with Garry's assistance changed his clothes and his bedding. I stood in the hallway crying. I didn't want Jaime to see me cry. Once the home care nurse left, I went to bed and cried all afternoon. My son Jessie came over and lay facing me in my bed for hours, while I repeated over and over, "I want my mom."

While lying together I told my son that when my mother was dying, she would call out for her mom and say, "There are times in your life when you just want your mom."

This said just as she was leaving me.

That night I return to the living room. For a time, I sit quietly holding Jaime's hand. Being in this small space with nowhere to go, we have been living in the liminal space between this world and the next. Words are not necessary but eventually I whisper to him, "I'm sorry. I was just so afraid, Jaime." He says, "Me too." No need for any more words. We have each other. We both know this. We return to our usual evening routine, which includes me asking him what he wants for dinner, knowing he will not be able to eat anything but that he likes to be asked, that he dreams of food.

The next day I am just waking up when Garry calls me into the living room. Jaime has made the change of worlds. His body is already growing cold. He has thrown up all over himself. Garry tells me he was there when it happened. Jaime knew it was time, and he had grabbed Garry's hand.

His last words were, "No, not now."

The doctor comes to declare him dead. She sits with us for a while. I am quiet, so quiet. She looks at me and says, "You knew, didn't you?" acknowledging the sadness I had carried alone for a week now. I knew his time was up and yet everyone around me had been acting as if everything was normal. My son had had a birthday party days before and I could not stay. I couldn't celebrate the birth of one son just as another was leaving. Some thought this selfish or that I was being overly emotional. No one understood that I was living with the demons of the past, the losses that had come before this one.

We make calls to everyone and ask the coroner to arrive at 4 p.m. We want some time with Jaime before they take him. Jessie changes Jaime's shirt. Later he tells me this moment haunts him. He had never touched a dead body before.

I clean up. Remove all evidence of sickness and create altars all around Jaime's body. He deserves that.

When the coroner comes, I am not ready to let him go, but I have no choice. It is time.

⁓

Anxiety has returned. I go to my doctor and he prescribes Ativan. I cannot attend Jaime's wake without it.

⁓

We decide to host the wake at the Charlatan, a gastropub Jaime and Jessie favoured. The day we go to see the place, I feel Jaime get into the back seat, his long, lanky legs bending to fit in the small space between my seat and his. I laugh. Of course, he wants to make sure we do this right.

The wake is what he would have wanted. There are so many people. A friend to many, he was like me, always collecting people who needed somewhere to belong. We have a table with all his games. He had asked us to tell his friends and family to take one game each, the one they most loved playing with him.

I spend most of the time in a booth with a couple of friends. I find it hard to talk to anyone else.

For months after the wake, I cannot leave the apartment. I try, but each time I get to the door, I cannot open it. On the rare occasions when I do manage to open the door, it feels as if there is an invisible force stopping me from crossing the threshold. Most days I just close the door, return to the living room where Jaime had died.

⁓

Thankfully, a few months later I am invited to Iceland to read. I have Ativan to relieve the anxiety. I am unable to travel with medical marijuana, so my doctor agrees to prescribe Percocet for the pain that never leaves my body. He feels this trip would be good for me.

I think, "I can do this. I need to do this." While there, I feel Jaime travelling with me. We stand together at the Althingi, a place familiar to us both as fans of *Game of Thrones*, which was partly filmed there.

The following year Garry's two sons take him to Ireland to visit their homeland. He says he felt Jaime travelling with him. That was our Jaime, always up for an adventure.

~

For several years after Jaime's death, whenever it is time to do a reading or presentation I have to take Ativan. Aware that it is risky for someone in recovery, I am careful not to overuse it. It is not easy. After years of freedom from a cluttered mind I am once again in the weeds with worry. It never ends, as all the accusations swirl in my head. *I should have done more to help Jaime. The world is not a safe place. You can do all the right things and still, bad things will happen to you.*

Most around me do not understand that I am falling apart, that some days I want to die.

~

I have not had a drink but feel as if I am coming back from a relapse when I return to my women's AA meetings at the Avalon Centre. While caring for Jaime, I had been unable to attend meetings.

The women in that room hold me tight. We all hold each other tight. We know the worst about each other, and we understand the need for forgiveness. We know that life can bring us more than we can handle if we try to go it alone.

~

Garry is not well. He is having pain in his abdomen and his blood work shows evidence of inflammation. A CT scan is ordered, and he has an appointment with an internal medicine specialist at St. Paul's Hospital. He is admitted that day. He has a mass in his abdomen; it is wrapped around his aorta and the passageways from his kidney to his bladder are closing. His kidney function is severely compromised. Different location, but the mass sounds similar to what happened to Jaime. One day he was fine and then he had a cough that wouldn't go away, so the doctor ordered X-rays of his lungs. The day he went for testing he received a call a few hours later. I believe it was the radiologist who said, "You need to go to the ER, right now." They could not see one lung. We all rushed to the ER and life was never the same. He had a mass wrapped around vital organs like his esophagus; it was inoperable. He was moved into the Cancer Agency where they began treatments that offered little hope of survival. Even though his doctor was "cautiously optimistic," I knew he was dying. For two long years I sat alone with this knowledge. People don't like to talk about these things. At least in my experience, they prefer to distance themselves from the possibility of death. Although Garry's mass was in a different location, it might be the same kind of cancer. To get a proper diagnosis they would need a biopsy, but a biopsy was too risky. This time I had no access to my own intuition. It was all too close. Fear interferes with our ability to receive guidance. For a time, we worried. Perhaps it was hereditary. Perhaps it was the same cancer that took our Jaime. In the end they landed on a presumptive diagnosis of a rare auto-immune disease that would require semi-annual treatments for the rest of his life. He would need to retire from a job he loved, but at least it didn't appear to be what took Jaime from us.

Oddly enough we learned in 2021 that Jaime is probably not a blood relative. This news came as a result of the DNA testing craze. It would appear that Jaime's father was not Garry's brother and that most likely there was a mix-up at the Meadow Lake Hospital in Saskatchewan. I had always felt that Jaime and I had some karmic bond, but I never imagined that the circuitous way he entered my life would involve babies being switched at birth.

Garry is in and out of hospital for the next year. It has been six months and loads of prednisone since he was last committed to hospital. We still do not have firm diagnosis.

During this year and a half, there have been many close calls. We nearly lost him more than once. Each time I am faced with the possibility of his death, I have had to make peace with the fact that I may soon be alone.

For fifteen years now, he has been my safe place; prior to him I had never known safety with a man. He is my lover, my partner in life. Not only has he been a father to my son; in a way he has been the father I never had, encouraging me to keep writing and providing a home soaked in safety. He has been the brothers I lost, siblings making our way in life together. He has become my best friend.

Just as I get the hang of this thing called love, I may lose it.

———

My sexy sax player sits next to me in the living room every night. We are like two birds on a wire. Even when he goes to bed, I feel him in that chair. For now, he is okay, we are okay, that is all we can ask for.

LOVE AS A RIVER

i

I used to long to be the poem you knew by heart
but now I long for sweaty sex

I miss the wordless places we could reach
two bodies pressing hard and fast

nothing held back

ii

my love now I can see
there is a river flowing between us
bringing the future forward
as the past moves out of sight
we are in a river of time

you with your sax
me in my chair
writing you this love poem

FLAT-FOOTED

I hear the words

allow your body to just be
ask nothing of it, breathe into
the bones of your feet

tender from the weight of sixty-five years
my feet need an apology
for those high-heeled days
toes squeezed into pointed places
narrowed into an arrow meant to land in men
the balls of my feet pressed against the earth
bringing pain I ignored until I couldn't

how I shamed my feet for what they needed
ignoring my flat-footed ways
arches that needed support
each night I would lie in bed
arthritic toes throbbing

I was never meant for heels
always happier in runners or
better yet workboots

but when the man of my dreams
bought me stilettos I caved

sober now he is going to save me
he makes a dinner reservation
I head to the tanning booth
a little overdone more red than brown
I wear the shoes he bought

I'd never been to the Hotel Vancouver
should have taken his hand
as I made my way to our table
where just in front of the buffet

I fall

      flat on my ass

HIS AND HERS

his ...

    to be invited and then uninvited
    to his grandson's birthday
    how long must one pay
    for youthful transgressions
    for not measuring up
    to expectations
    forged in late-night chats
    with girlfriends
    before texting
    before email
    before he knew better

hers ...

    no one wants to know her body aches
    her shoes are not a fashion statement
    that words, without a home, linger on her tongue
    between dreams a dampening has taken place
    there is a garden path between them
    his love now expressed in the form of a cheque

theirs ...

    between them there is enough regret to go around
    there are the blameless   grandchildren   victims
    of a crime no one committed
    but all witnessed

LOVE IN THE TIME OF COVID

my body remembers
the shape of your mouth
the lingering on lips
the days when we were receptive
to one another and we merged
two becoming one thought

we had both sensed need until need became needy
but we soon learned returning to the same well
muddied our inner waterways
and yet we could not stop returning
to the hope of more
afraid to ask why
we keep trying until
our bones ached with longing
until we wanted no more

today we take our place at the dining room table
glance at one another with gratitude
together we look towards uncertainty and
a Christmas wrapped in COVID restrictions

in this masked world
we are learning to smile with our eyes
and that some days we only have one another

DOPPELGÄNGERS

month one

> masks – food delivery
> doctor appointments fill our days until
> a couple of imposters sit in our living room
> evil twins whispering dread
> remote control between them
>
> real-life examples of what not to do
> we are witnesses to panic emptying
> toilet-paper shelves

>   we stock up   try to stay indoors

month two

> alone together too much
> we begin to feed on one another
> tethered to distractions we say
> we do not leave the house
> but there are sightings in grocery store aisles
> where snack food and popcorn kernels
> were quietly abducted
> when out we wear masks   wash our hands
> within this container of safety   no viruses can enter
> and yet we are contaminated   mirror images
> spitting kernels into bowls of disdain dished up by
> a little too much closeness
> each day on social media we offer versions of ourselves
> we become two with different stories re: the same day
> unintentional participants in exposure therapy
> there is an unveiling of thin skin and a turning to online others
> where too many disclosure displays leave us both diminished
> no longer tethered to the tangible
> we have become someone we no longer recognize
> physical sensations noted until they aren't
> day after day we sit numb   side by side
>   the remote between us

>   we stock up   try to stay indoors

month three

    decisions are made re TV viewing habits
    more shows about artists and the music of our youth
    I can feel the dread emptying out of me
    pouring itself onto the carpet
    into glasses of coffee and all over the kitchen counter

                we stock up   try to stay indoors

month four

    we buy a Netflix membership
    binge-watch *Stranger Things*
    three seasons in two days
    seeing ourselves in the doppelgängers
    a decision is made to post positive
    to remember who we are and which side we want to feed
    while others return to their habits
    phase three does not include us
    we remain ghosts repeating the Serenity Prayer
    at sixty-five and seventy we wonder will we ever be free

                we stock up   try to stay indoors

SOFT GAZE

I had something to tell you
it seemed to matter
almost urgent but then
you smiled and it was gone

why do we nurse hurts
ignore the good
there are teachings that say
we should try "to see each other new"
to think of each moment as precious
worth protecting

I was taught not to carry forward
the baggage of the old
of who you were yesterday
aware my thoughts can interfere
with your unfolding

I remember to soften my gaze
allow you the dignity of space to learn
yet this is so hard to do without trust
without a history to refer to

I had something to tell you
it seemed to matter
almost urgent but then
you smiled and it was all gone

Beside a Well:
Walking with Women

Beside a well, one won't thirst; beside a sister,
one won't despair.

—NÜSHU TEXT

As a young woman, I did not like the roles assigned to women
and often wished that I had been born a boy. I wanted to do all
the things that boys got to do, things like working with metal and
wood in shop. I wanted to play hockey but, in those days, girls
didn't play hockey and we had to take home economics, not shop.
We were to learn how to be good wives, but I did not want to be
a wife. I purposely coasted through cooking and sewing classes,
doing the minimum – just enough to pass.

I did not want to learn how to type. I wasn't going to be a
secretary, either. I wasn't going to bring some man his coffee and
take his notes.

I had watched my mother wait on my father, ironing his clothes,
warming the car up for him, making sure dinner was on the table
at the time he designated. I did not see these things as acts of love
but rather as subservience, and I was allergic to subservience.

I wondered why women like my mother accepted life as "the
wife." Looking back I see that she was quietly resisting wherever
she could. She had a life outside our house; as the president of
the women's group at our church, she organized teas and raised
money for the church doing craft fairs. She also took courses and
went back to work as a licensed practical nurse at Tuxedo Villa.
Four children and yet she managed to have a life of her own. A life
I sometimes was included in – as her only girl, I was her assistant
when she hosted the church teas and craft sales. She wanted her
patients in the nursing home to have visitors so would ask me
to come see her at work. She said many were lonely. Some were
distant and others would clap their hands in delight or chuckle,
exclaiming, "You're Lorraine's daughter." Mom would kiss them
on the forehead or cheek. She always told me that she worried for
the Filipino care aides, saying that she didn't like the way some

of the other nurses and doctors treated them. She hosted their wedding and baby showers in our home.

—

I have always felt the need for solidarity with women. This began with my mother. At times we were more like sisters. She could be such a girlie girl – something I was not but liked to be around.

We enjoyed each other's company. I got to do lots of things that my brothers did not. Things like tea on the porch after the boys had gone to bed. Staying up late and being the one she talked to about Dad made me feel special. Grown-up. She needed me; I liked that.

Sometimes she would take me shopping with her and to do tasks, like paying the bills. In those days we paid bills by cheque, and even though my father made good money, when he needed alcohol, he would write cheques at the local bar. This often meant the cheques to pay our rent or mortgage, utilities, the milkman, and the gas station bounced. Most paydays were spent repairing the damage, and this fell to my mom. I would go with her to take cash or certified cheques to anyone we owed money.

Mom always dressed up for these occasions. I imagine this was in hopes of maintaining some dignity. I could see she was embarrassed, but she wouldn't give in to feeling sorry for herself. As she prepared to enter buildings filled with people who probably judged her, she would turn, wink at me and say, "I'll be right back." She never said it, but I knew she was jokingly inferring that she was using sex to pay what we owed. This was particularly funny to my teenage self because it was quite out of character for her. My mom was a modest woman who often used jokes to defuse situations, to make us kids feel like everything would be all right.

—

My longest friendship began as an act of solidarity. I was fifteen and seeing the school James Dean. Laurie was in a different school and just fourteen when I found out we were dating the same guy. Armed with this knowledge, I introduced myself to her in the washroom at a dance. She was a beauty in those hot pants with her black hair that went all the way to her bum. She was dark-skinned like me.

We both broke up with him that night. We didn't blame the guy for trying to juggle two girls, but we weren't having it.

We have been close friends since that first night when I told her that her bad boy was also seeing me.

———

Both Laurie and I thought we were "part Native." Later in life we applied to the St. Boniface Historical Society to get our genealogies done. While they informed me that I had far more Indigenous ancestry than I'd ever known, they could not locate any of Laurie's Indigenous Ancestors. This mystified us both, given she looked even more "Native" than I did.

I consider her my sister, and even though I am a year older, she is the big sister. When I go to Winnipeg, it is with her and her husband Terry that I stay, not my original family.

We have lived completely different lives: hers one of stability, in which she has been married to Terry for nearly fifty years. I was the maid of honour at their wedding. She worked for the federal government and Terry worked for CN Rail. They never left Charleswood. I could not wait to get out. I never felt like I fit. Laurie is the only one I stayed in touch with from my high school days.

I have had many jobs and moved around a lot. Not just from city to city but also, wherever I lived, I was never one to stay in one place or one relationship for very long. My first marriage lasted four years. My second didn't even make it to two.

Despite our differences, Laurie and I have an inexplicable connection. She always says that she knew right away that I was one of "her people." Over the years there have been times we didn't talk for a while, but we have always returned to one another and when we do, we just pick up where we left off.

It has been a fifty-one-year conversation, admittedly a little one-sided at times. I was always in crisis. She would be there to listen and when appropriate offer guidance. I probably wouldn't be here today were it not for her kindness.

My other closest friend was another West Coast transplant and ex-Winnipegger, She Who Saved Me, the woman I met at the Maple Ridge treatment centre, the astrologer who predicted Jessie's birth and who had also predicted that I would find success as an author later in life. She was and still is a wonder to me. Like a tree in the wind, she was rooted in Taurus energy. Always animated, her arms would wave wildly as she held court at our local vegetarian restaurant, Greens and Gourmet.

It was She Who Saved Me who introduced me to chanting, meditation, and our guru, the same guru mentioned in the book *Eat, Pray, Love: One Woman's Search for Everything across Italy, India and Indonesia,* which was made into a movie. Our walks on the Stanley Park Seawall sustained me in my early sobriety. She was the first to hold my son Jessie. He is named after her grandmother.

Generous with her gifts, she would read my tarot cards and tell me what was going on with my transits every year. When I was in labour, she kept whispering in my ear, "He needs to come soon. We need his moon to be in Cancer."

She knew this would be a bond between me and my son. He made it on time, and I will never know for sure if it is his moon in Cancer that made the difference for us. I do know that he and I are well suited. We belong together. Mother and son, we are close.

I wanted sisters and found some along the way. I also longed for a daughter.

I found her working at Sweet Cherubim, where my son and I ate frequently. Zofia had just started working there and was newly in town from Chilliwack. She and Jessie had entered that circling stage where potential lovers decide how deep their interest is in one another.

The first time we met, I was struck by how much she looked like my younger self. As I watched her work, I smiled to myself, thinking how often we are attracted to people like our parents. I could not help but notice her vulnerability as she excitedly told me about being Carrier and that she had recently moved to Vancouver. Just out of foster care, she was couch-surfing and had no cellphone. She could not afford to take the bus, so for every shift she would walk eight kilometres to work. I worried for her safety. I knew what it is like to be alone, to have no one to turn to.

After hearing her story, the mother bear in me grew restless. I had to do something, but what could I do? I sat eating my food, watching her wait on customers, when suddenly I heard that still-small voice. "Ask her out for a coffee. You need to get her a cellphone." At first I argued quietly inside my head, "No way. She'll think I'm creepy or nuts." But the voice became more insistent. I gave in and headed to the counter, taking a deep breath before asking, "Would you like to have a coffee one day?" She seemed a little caught off guard but did say yes.

Prior to getting together, I researched cellphone plans and suggested we meet at a coffee shop next to the cellphone provider I had decided on. We weren't rich, but she was vulnerable, and her safety was important.

I had just finished doing research about all the Murdered and Missing Indigenous Women, Girls, and Two-Spirits (MMIWG2S) for an article in the *First Nation Drum* newspaper. I also knew from my own life how dangerous life can be for Indigenous women. A cellphone would be a necessity. But would she agree to let me do this? I was about to find out.

Once we had the cellphone in hand, I asked her to put my phone number in there first. "You can call me anytime." That was ten years ago. There have been many tears and plenty of joy since then.

At first, every time we got together, I would drop her off at the end of our visit and watch her enter homes that worried me. Each time I could not drive away until I took a moment to sit in my car and sob. I was so afraid for her, but I was not her mother, and besides, she didn't need someone telling her how to live. She was making the best of the options that were available to her. Many days I wished I had a spare bedroom and could have her live with us.

Given our histories, trust was not easy for either of us. Early on I decided that if I did this, I would wait for her, no matter how much time it took for her to understand that I was a safe person for her to lean into. She had been abandoned over and over again. The effects of this abandonment were apparent.

I tried to do the things my mom did with me. I took her shopping, thinking this would be a fun girl thing to do. I wanted her to feel special the way my mom would make me feel special when we did things together.

I could see that she did not share in my excitement. Later, when we talked about it, she told me that shopping for clothes, as a foster child, had never been a pleasant experience. No one cared what she wanted, and they always looked for the cheapest things. Shopping had been a shame-filled event.

Just the other day, she texted me a photo of a pair of Doc Martens she was buying at one of the shoe stores we had gone to in those early days. I had bought her a pair of Doc Martens then, just like the ones I wanted but didn't feel I could afford. Now here she was proudly purchasing her own shoes and wanting to share the experience with me.

Zofia and Jessie only had one date. They are more like brother and sister today, and the truth is we might all be related. I have a Tse'khene great-great-great-grandmother, Nancy McDougall, and the Carrier Nations and the Tse'khene are very close. They are all part of the Carrier Sekani Tribal Council, which represents seven Nations. Today Zofia describes herself as Dakelh and Polish. Like me she is biracial, but she has Indian Status through the Nak'azdli Whut'en First Nation. We both have many relatives in the Fort St. James area.

One day I hope to get her genealogy done so we can see if we are, in fact, related. One thing I know for sure is that her Ancestors and my Ancestors wanted us to meet and to care for one another. It was they who whispered in my ear that first time we met.

Zofia is a singer/songwriter now, a poet, and a radio-show host. We intend to write a book together one day, a weaving of our parallel life experiences.

For many years she called me her "Spirit Momma." She has thankfully been reunited with her biological mother. I'm grateful that her mother, Josephine, is willing to share her with me.

There are so many women who have walked with me over the years. Some of them only walked with me for a short time, others for most of my lifetime. Few are as dear to me as my friend and Elder, Sharon Jinkerson-Brass.

Sharon and I met when I was working with PeerNetBC co-facilitating training for peer-support facilitators at Native Health. That Sharon is a Saulteaux Elder should come as no surprise; it has always been the Anishinaabeg who have welcomed me and whose teachings I feel most comfortable leaning into.

Sharon had worked in palliative care and was of great support when we walked Jaime home. One time in particular stands out. Caring for a dying child in a one-bedroom apartment while living with fibromyalgia was exhausting. In part this was because Jaime had come to us angry and afraid. At first he would not accept any help but was too weak to leave. When I reached out to Sharon, she said, "I know. I have seen it. It is always the angry ones who take so long to leave." Like all wise ones, she said no more. I understood that it fell to me to help him make peace with all that he had lost.

A Sixties Scoop survivor, Sharon carries the wisdom of her grandmother. She is a Pipe Carrier. We talk often about Ceremony and the need to be responsive. We recognized something in each other the first time we met. Perhaps she could feel my Ancestors. Perhaps she could see I needed an Elder.

Even though she is younger than me, she is one of my Elders. I felt blessed when she invited me to a Ceremony to honour the Matriarchs of the Vancouver Downtown Eastside. In this Ceremony we were each gifted with a cedar umbilical cord and told that the Saulteaux would bury their umbilical cords.

For some time, I thought I would return to my homeland and bury the cedar umbilical cord in the place I was born, Portage la Prairie, in Treaty 1 Territory (Manitoba).

But that never happened.

⁓

When Sharon heard that I was part Icelandic, she told me that she was from one of the Saulteaux Nations that had been nearly wiped out when the Icelanders brought smallpox to the Gimli area. Learning what the Icelanders had brought to Sharon's people, some of whom might be my people as well, left me wondering how I could make amends. I could see that our meeting, just like the one with Zofia, was about the unfinished business of our Ancestors. For several years after being gifted with the cedar umbilical cord, I laid tobacco and prayed asking how I could bring healing to our communities, to our Ancestors.

On my one and only trip to Iceland in 2017, I took that cedar umbilical cord with me. It was my custom to bring it to readings, as it contained Medicines and the reminder of the beauty and strength of those fifty Matriarchs of the Downtown Eastside.

I was in Iceland to do a reading from the *Contemporary Verse 2* (*CV2*) issue entitled "Convergence" about the Icelanders' arrival on Turtle Island.

This trip truly was a convergence for me. While in Iceland I realized that I needed to bury the cedar umbilical cord there. When I told angela rawlings, a Canadian poet living in Iceland, about this revelation she suggested we go to a black-sand beach, where the Grótta Island Lighthouse sits on a peninsula that points to Turtle Island. It seemed the perfect place to bury the cord. She picked me up the next day and when we arrived at the parking lot she said, "Hold onto your door!" The wind was so strong that it would easily rip the door off. It was bitterly cold. The burying of the cord was a little more rushed than I had imagined. With angela as my sacred witness, I said a brief prayer asking for healing for my Ancestors and for Sharon's and buried the cord. As soon as this was done, I could feel a shift in my body. It was as if my Métis and Icelandic blood flowed with more ease throughout my body. No longer compartmentalized, they had merged.

⁓

I have always been attracted to the unusual, to people who walk their own path. It was Betsy Warland who gave me a name for this, and the understanding of why this was. I am "a person of between." As a person of between, I relate to all other persons of between, and Betsy is no exception. She and her partner ingrid rose were my first writing mentors. Being bookended between these two has allowed me not only to grow as a writer and a writing mentor, but also as a woman.

When the two of them first got together, they looked at one another and said, "Whoever sees her first needs to tell her ... we are a couple now." This news did make me nervous at first. In the past, being friends with couples had not gone well for me. When they would fight, I would begin to feel like that little girl whose momma needed her protection. I would feel like I had to choose, take a side. Over the years, Betsy and ingrid have shown me that there need not be any triangulation. There is room for everyone.

⁓

Many times it has been the women in my life who have kept me going. With some I have walked the labyrinth at St. Paul's Anglican Church, in Vancouver, and in the summer months we go to Jericho Beach, where we draw a labyrinth in the sand. Time and time again we enter sacred space together, women leaning into prayer and the invisible forces that sustain us.

It has been the Indigenous and non-Indigenous women in my life who have been there to quench my thirst for the sacred and to walk with me.

⁓

Many of the poems in this collection were written while in ingrid rose's "writing from the body" workshops. Most of the women are Crones, over sixty, some over eighty. We have taken many deep dives into our bodies and surfaced with our fingers filled with words as we write and rewrite our stories.

These are women who have known loss. A number of them are widows.

⁓

Garry still has no diagnosis. He was close to leaving more than once, but he continues to resist the journey to the other side. We both want more time together. We are just getting the hang of this love thing.

I turn to prayer, ask for help, for the right person to lean into so that I can stay strong and be there for him.

I find her. She is a healer. One who has also known loss. During our third session, she asks me to consider that "the world is a friendly place." Such an odd thing to say to a survivor. Even so I can feel my entire body relax each time she repeats this phrase. After all that has gone wrong, this is a hard thing to believe, but I must.

⁓

COVID is making life difficult. Garry and I have been alone together in this six-hundred-square-foot apartment for a full year now. I decide to use my Canadian Tire points to buy some Christmas lights for our balcony.

Once, at the Marine Way Market, I stop in at McDonald's for a sausage and an Egg McMuffin. As I cross the parking lot, McMuffin in hand, a crow follows me. He is a cheeky fellow. I can tell he wants some of my food so I ask him, "Is this what you want?" He nods and comes closer. I throw him some sausage, my favourite part, but heck, he could probably use some protein too. He hops towards the offering. Soon there are others.

I keep pinching off small pieces and throwing them to the crows until a sea gull arrives. He is aggressive, but the crows are equally insistent on getting their fair share.

Soon I feel like I am in a scene from *The Birds*. It is all too much. I begin to feel afraid, so I head for Canadian Tire. The birds are in pursuit. I feel silly, fear grows in my belly. I walk faster and faster. I really hope no one is looking. Once under the overhang of the store, safe from dive-bombing, I laugh at myself. There was nothing to be afraid of.

Maybe the world really is a friendly place. Maybe the worst is behind me.

THE MANY FACES OF THE GODDESS

some toboggan their way
straight arrows seeking the suburbs
where tales of magic kitchens
home births and placenta promises

        call them home to motherhood

others weave their way through bodies
all sizes   shapes   orientations
willing to grind and glide
until groans become whimpers

        spirited sorceresses they enchant all

some cluster in corners of the internet
seeking safety in numbers
they create Twitter-thread clans
shield-maidens of the internet

        always there to reassure one another

some are brave trans women unfurling
fearless in pursuit of the divine, the feminine
sadly accustomed to the sharp words of exclusion from
those who don the armour of good intentions

        they open our eyes to possibility

some dream velvet
their jewellery boxes filled
with crystals confirming the truth
they have been bewitched
ensorcelled by offerings from holy men
they have become metaphysical Barbies
filling themselves with possibility

        until one day the Goddess within awakens

some head to the gym
their spandex status seeking
takes them to health clubs where deep breathing
hot yoga promises profound change

their aerobic efforts rewarded
with hard bodies   strong hearts

they model self-care   until they don't

while others sit in chairs on cruise decks
their closets filled with velour track suits
their stretchy-pant lives
elastic in nature allow for expansion
every direction purple excess
prosperity found in abundance

always room for more growth

some prefer serpentine dreaming
their bodies a watery plea
if they were fish they would be pickerel
young again swimming

all chakras cleared

others hold space

their circadian ways uncomplicated   incorruptible
they weave a life without guilt   they refuse to carry shame

their uncluttered bodies homes for the sacred

TOGETHER WE WALK THE LABYRINTH

in this shared silence
there are rounded corners
where bodies circle circles
within circles   our bodies fluid
opening to each other we become
rounded corners   no sharp turns here

      only prayers filling the walls
        filling our hearts

once at the centre we wait
eyes closed we feel bodies passing
bodies turning in the softening
of rounded corners

      one foot in front of the other
      we walk towards peace

in the background the faint sounds of piano keys
the chords of our longing have become a song
our pain put on pause
some left in the rounded corners
where the softening edges
the sound of the piano
show us another way through
the maze of emotions each day brings

      heads bowed we give thanks
      for the healing the circling brings

together we walk
in this prayer-filled room
a place where many are answered
all outside sounds muted by meditation
even if jarring they become music

turning us inward
moving us away
from resistance

      minds emptied

we retrace our steps

our bodies filled with light we walk
in the quiet of our yearning for stillness
our questions answered   we are nourished
it will now be easier to lead with love
and when we forget

eyes closed we will remember
the sharing of silence
the walk towards peace

FALLING

gliding over the edge
a woman becomes a waterfall
falling earthbound

she knows she was never meant to fly
her feet belong on the ground
but she does prefer the height

the excitement of the cliff
so climbs back up
once there she again flings herself over the edge

becomes the waterfall falling
after many climbs and descents
she becomes purified mist

now she can float
now she is happy
her body feels light

she is no longer falling
she has learned to float

CRONE WISDOM

visited by the dark strangers

who ask a thousand questions

she seeks a large map

delights in following her fingers

comes to her own lake

head   bent down

   dark eyes fixed upon

         bevelled glass

she casts a circle recites blessings

       fills with visions

samples the fruit

          avoids the apples

IN THE WANDERING

within wet wildness a woman not of this world winds her way
within the in and out breath   until a deepening occurs
her bodied ways of being birth wildling children
who cannot be trusted to carry the slippery words
of those who do not speak with the trees
of those who do not love water

her wildling children wanderers – all of them
wind their way through breath – in then out
as they seek what lies beneath it all
they do not look up to a God in the sky
· they seek the Goddesses, the ones who find solace in mud huts
the same Goddesses who know time spent wandering is potent

WOMEN FIND WAYS

The language that women speak when no one is there to correct them.

—HÉLÈNE CIXOUS

"Coming to Writing" and Other Essays (1986)

look at the script
see bird tracks
crows walking
deliberately down
elegant calligraphy
this ancient script has a genealogy
bone etchings of belonging
seeded in the language
carved for the Goddess
women and birds interchangeable

women thought illiterate whispered
shape-shifting inscriptions
inside the slippers that bound their feet

it was a way that women could speak

I'M IN ICELAND, DARLING

they have poetry in the bathroom
uncredited text on blocks of wood
cheeky commentaries on life
some chilling reminders
those who live on shifting ground
take their poetry seriously

it is Christmas in the mall   red everywhere
silver adornments for trees and tabletops
I find a coffee shop   listen to words I do not understand
but feel familiar   I want to lean in
I do not know if my grandmother spoke these words
I do not know if I have heard this before
all I know is that I am leaning into her
and everywhere I go I look for her face

I find her at a dinner party
she is pretty   I am glad
would she have been single too
a photographer   not a farmer with seventeen children
this apartment could have been hers
the old furniture   the artwork passed down
my grandmother had nothing to give me but love
and a cheque for $200   carefully noted in her will
the cost of diaspora long forgotten
there are no accounting methods
to track what was lost   language the first to go
the passing down of heirlooms   carvings filled
with the stories once in the hands of the maker
living on in the wood   tellings of another sort

my grandmother's mother came with nothing   not even a mother
her father reluctant to claim her   listed as nanny
not daughter   not sister   her mother lost
went missing in the country where we take a drive

I look for her   but she is not there
I am here to be a witness to the past
I stand where my Ancestors once stood

outdoor governing   a gathering place
named Althingi

here the land   the little people honoured

                    a short walk
                    waters dark
                      deep
                 we share a coin
                  make a wish

the land is filled with silence
yet it never stops talking
tells me it knows me   I belong to its past
the pristine snow and the heat of the earth
bring geyser remembrances
the gushing of watery words made white-hot
by those who do not live brown
my skin erupts   steam escapes from my mouth

        I feel the burning

the lava words of my aunties and uncles
the way they slow crawl just below my skin

        I am a volcano   on an island

          I become my own island

I have always been between
the wombs of my grandmothers
offered two worlds   one with circles
where we lay ourselves open
to the warmth of a fire
the other a burning of another sort
both sides made strong by storytelling
by connection to the Lands of their Ancestors
each a reflection of circumstances
black-sand beaches   sharp   salt
cold water   peninsulas pointing to Canada
where voyagers from both sides ventured
both sides made strong by storytelling

and a place called Turtle Island

IN THE MIRROR

> *rounder than the moon*
> *and far more faithful*

—LUCILLE CLIFTON

"song at midnight," *The Collected Poems*
of Lucille Clifton, 1965–2010 (2012)

i

when did mirrors become something to avoid?
there was a time my reflection
offered assurances of acceptability
attractive enough for special attention
I could tell myself everything will be okay
but age has left me with thinning greying hair
very little colour there or on my cheeks
don't get me started on my belly
bigger than when pregnant
I am now what my father called a "lard-ass"

ii

there was an adjustment period
between forty then fifty and now sixty
I no longer avoid mirrors nor seek them out
I no longer need to know what I look like
when I do see my reflection I am reassured

with age comes grace

but only if you want it

Movement:
Bodies and Boundaries

I have heard it said that illness is an attempt to escape the truth. I suspect it is actually an attempt to embody the whole truth, to remember all of ourselves.

—KAT DUFF

The Alchemy of Illness (1993)

My muscle pain has reached new levels. My doctor recommends massage therapy. I look for a massage therapist close to home. I have learned the hard way that sometimes a long drive home undoes all the good done on the massage table. Google searches reveal a place within walking distance. I examine the photos on their website, search the faces of all the practitioners, hoping for a woman. Instead, I find a young man who has a friendly face. I am surprised that he is the one I am drawn to. After all that has happened, I am cautious about letting men touch me. In fact, at sixty-six years of age I still cross the street if I come upon a man when I am alone ... but this man seems safe. I book an appointment.

~

My massage therapist and I talk while he works on me. He tells me about his relationship and his life as a boy. Like most healers, he has a history. But his hands ... oh my Goddess. Everything he touches opens. I feel my muscles relax, and places I did not know existed in my body are awakening. Sometimes his touch releases a memory that causes tears.

I have been here before. I spent years doing visceral manipulation with another healer. She would always say the same thing when I would cry just as a cellular memory was being dislodged. "This one is a very old memory." She never offered more than that, and I would not get much information with these memories, but I could feel how deep some of my pain went. There was always more.

~

On my third visit to the massage therapist, he touches my hip bone and suddenly I hear a child's voice. I open my eyes and my

179

inner child is standing at the end of the massage table. I am so small. They say I always ate like a bird. Truth was I was too sad to eat most days.

I am startled by the clarity of this vision. It feels so real. I am both the one on the table and a piece of me, my inner child, outside my body. She stands with her wee hand on the massage table. Even she doesn't want to be in this body.

I want to comfort myself as I am crying. Some memory is being released. The "little one," as my step-grandfather Fred the fireman would call me, says, "I don't want to be afraid anymore." I know what she means. I have been afraid my entire life. This has to change.

I promise her I will take better care of her. I will stop asking her to do things that frighten her. I tell her I won't let anyone close to her that she is not comfortable with.

⁓

Today I learned about the unmarked graves of two hundred and fifteen little ones found by the Tk'emlúps te Secwépemc First Nation at the Kamloops Indian Residential School. This revelation falls on the heels of reading *Rooster Town: The History of an Urban Métis Community, 1902–1961*, a book about the Métis community on the outskirts of Winnipeg that was once "a place of cultural safety within the hostile, white-settler, urban environment." "Hostile" is a strong word, and sadly it still applies in many settings where as Indigenous we do not feel welcome. As children our small bodies breathe in the words of others. And even if not articulated, how people see us does matter. We can feel their disdain.

When young and working in Winnipeg, I was often asked what I was. I knew why they asked. I had dark hair and my skin was darker than that of the other employees. In those days it was always a man asking, hoping I would say I was Spanish or something that would fulfill his fantasy of the Exotic Other. I was cheeky, not interested in playing into their need for this so would respond with "Indian" or "part Native." Once older the question persisted, only now I would say "Métis." I have years of experience with the awkward silence and the shift that would take place on the faces of most who asked. I could feel many of them file me under the "always late, loose woman, dirty, drunk, and not reliable" category.

These days I am rarely asked, and when I am there are those who are looking for an "Indian friend." Others want to know if I am a "pretendian." To be honest I am not sure what is worse. It all feels dehumanizing, othering, and sets up expectations I have no desire to fulfill.

Like many people of colour, I have had to work against the prejudice and systemic barriers that were placed in my way. But at least as a child I got to go to bed in my own home, with my own parents each night, and my father made sure I lived in a safe neighbourhood.

The complexity and the irony of his decision to build our home in Charleswood, an upper-middle-class part of Winnipeg, a place where I did not feel like I belonged, is something I am still unpacking. My father's reasons were made clearer to me as I read about what happened to Rooster Town and contemplated the effects of residential schools. I knew both he and his family had faced racism. I knew from my uncle Clarence Campeau that he too never felt like he belonged in either the white world or the Indigenous one. Clarence would tell me "neither side wants us," and that this was why he was so devoted to bettering the circumstances of his Métis brothers and sisters. When young he had lived on the road allowance near Archerwill, Saskatchewan, on the Land of the Blackfoot / Niitsítapi ᖹᐟᒧᐧᒣᑯ, Métis, Anishinaabeg ᐊᓂᔑᓈᐯᒃ, Cree, and Očhéthi Šakówiŋ. Just like the residents of Rooster Town, his family had been forced to give up their homes and had nowhere to go. At least not anywhere they were welcome. Being forced to disperse and assimilate further left him without the support of his community. It was he who encouraged me to claim my Métis "status," as he called it in those days. It was his stepdaughter, my cousin Bernie, who confirmed that my grandmother was indeed Métis. A few years later, when having my genealogy done by the St. Boniface Historical Society, I learned that my long-dead grandfather was also Métis, and that we had many land scrips in our direct lineage. Even knowing this, it has been very hard to know my place in the Indigenous world.

So many people speak about coming back to community and the need to reclaim teachings, language, and culture, but what they never mention is how long this process takes and how complicated it is. There is so much pain in all of us and sometimes it comes out as lateral violence. Those of us coming back make mistakes. Unaware of Protocols and in need of Elders, we don't always feel welcomed. In my case this has been further complicated by the fact that I haven't lived in my homeland since 1983. Sadly, my health often prevents me from participating in events and ceremonies provided by the local Métis or other Indigenous Nations.

There is a litany of words used to describe those of us who were not raised with our culture or who are seen as falling short of some ideal Indigeneity. As a young woman, I heard terms like "apple": red on the outside and white on the inside. Having a white mother and being named after my Icelandic grandmother, I was under the influence of whiteness. Both women were kind, community-minded, spiritual women and had much to teach me. Given this it was hard for my young self to understand why it was not okay to be like them, and the expectation that I be "all in" about Indigeneity is still confusing to me. I am, after all, "part white," but we didn't say that. We said "part Native." All I knew then was that I didn't feel white and was frequently asked what I was. Clearly the world didn't see me as white. But as with many Métis, no one wanted to talk about this. It was my mother who told me that my father hated being "Native." She cautioned me against bringing it up. Everyone wanted me to just let it go, but I could not.

Once I knew my lineage, it was clear that the stories I had been told were not true. I have many Indigenous Ancestors from many different Nations. In more recent generations, it has been Métis marrying Métis. Since I was a young child in the forest in Goose Bay, I have heard their voices. When I first started meditating, I remember having visions of men in suede coats with fringes and muskets strategizing a rebellion. This vision came to me long before I knew the story of the Métis.

It was an act of resistance to claim my Métis citizenship. I did it for all my Métis Ancestors. I am happy to say that I started a trend in my family. As I shared our stories, my one living brother and many cousins took interest; many have gotten their Métis citizenship.

~~~

My first book, *page as bone – ink as blood*, came out just as Joseph Boyden's claims to Indigenous identity were coming under scrutiny. As a Métis still sorting out my own ancestry, what I witnessed shook me. I was angry that he had said he was Métis, a term that has been misused by many. Given this, I could forgive his confusion. At one time it was commonly said that there were capital-*M* Métis, those like me who could trace their lineage back to the Red River Settlement, and then there were those that were small-*m* Metis, who were simply "part Native." Our identity is still under discussion, and sadly there are many who have no one to claim them. To have people like Joseph claiming to be Métis was not helping any of us. Now every Métis was suspect. Since that time, I have witnessed the many attempts to sort us all into the appropriate categories. Painful as this is to witness, I do understand the need to protect what little space is carved out for Indigenous writers in the literary and academic worlds.

Some people do have questionable ancestry, but in many cases this is not entirely their fault. Information and connections were lost long before they were born. I can tell you that witnessing the takedown of those deemed not Indigenous enough still sends shivers down my spine. No wonder my father was so afraid of claiming his ancestry. Claiming his Indigeneity did not come with any guarantees of backing from his First Nations counterparts. He must have decided it was safer to just say he was French.

Thankfully this is changing, and we Métis are not only reclaiming our place on Turtle Island but also many of our First Nations brothers and sisters are welcoming us. We are being included in Land acknowledgments where appropriate. This gives me hope.

I now look at my father so differently and wish I had known how to help him heal. I take comfort in the fact that as I gathered the stories about our Ancestors and shared them with him, he made the decision to come out of hiding and claim his Métis citizenship. Sadly, he died before the paperwork was submitted.

Today I attended a Ceremony for the two hundred and fifteen little ones. The orange T-shirts, the Medicines, the drumming and singing all bring me some peace. As one who has witnessed and experienced violence in my childhood home, I've shed many tears for these little ones. Knowing that they suffered even more, and that their parents never knew what happened to them, feels unbearable.

One of the Elders at the Ceremony spoke about the fact that his father discouraged them from speaking their language. He was told, "We weren't going to get anywhere being 'Indian.'" When he said this, I thought of my grandmother and all my Métis relatives who believed this was true and left their language and culture behind. Another Elder talked about the year-long "wiping of the tears" Ceremony, and once again I was struck by the chasm that exists between the two worlds, worlds that I have been straddling my whole life. The colonized world seems so cold to me. Three days off if a loved one dies, and so many of us grieve alone. We have funeral services where the only fires lit are those of the crematorium.

I and many other survivors have health issues. Our bodies flooded with stress hormones, we struggle with inflammation and pain. Our overloaded nervous systems respond in ways that make life hard. The wearing down of the body aligns with the wearing down of our spirit. There are the very traumatic events, like those I experienced with my father and with Dean, and then there are the daily microaggressions. I am not a scientist or doctor, but I have lived with this body for sixty-six years and have been a witness to its decline. I know I am not alone. There are many like me who struggle. Most of us are empathic and trying to find a way to live in a world where emotions are discounted. Some days I think we are the canaries in the mines.

As a survivor I have had to learn to manage my mind and, as one spiritual teacher said, treat it like a three-year-old child. He taught me that it was up to me to redirect my mind towards the soothing and uplifting, just as one would redirect a child away from something harmful. I know that for a time this can work, but when under stress, the flashbacks, the repetitive shaming thoughts, can come rushing back. This does not mean we shouldn't try or that these teachings are not valid. All it means is that we are never done. We are never fully healed. We can, however, learn to live with the limitations that may come with caring for a body and a spirit that has been harmed in ways that leave deep ruts and well-travelled roadways back to pain. Just as an alcoholic can learn to live without alcohol, we can learn to live a more peaceful life.

I do many things each day to soothe my spirit. I light candles. I take walks in Queen's Park, where I can talk to the trees, lay tobacco, and feel at peace. I surround myself with gentler people, especially since that little one presented herself at the end of my massage table. She was letting me know that she had had enough. She needed me to set firmer boundaries and to not let harsher folk close. None of this was news but what made it different was that I felt her fear and could see her fragility, something I had not wanted to acknowledge in myself.

I am fragile and that is okay. I did not cause this. It is part of being not only a survivor but an empath. It comes with the territory, so rather than try to change who I am it would be best if I not only accepted this fact but also celebrated it as the gift it is. It is, after all, what makes me a good poet, a good mother, a good life partner and friend.

—

I know many young ones blame us baby boomers for where we all find ourselves, including some youth in the Indigenous community who feel let down by those who came before them. One recent tweet from a young Indigenous artist said that we had bought into the idea that being polite would work. I would not disagree. Many of us were sold what some call "respectability politics." Our clothes, our hair, our manners monitored daily by parents, teachers, and caregivers who thought living white and/or hiding our ways was our best possible option. We were told that if we worked hard, we too could be successful. We were told that if we went to school, we could get good jobs, be homeowners. Some of us did get good jobs and are homeowners but many of us floundered within the limitations that sexism, racism, homophobia, and other forms of discrimination brought into our lives.

We were sold a lie, one that does not acknowledge systemic barriers or that there are other ways to live. We have a lot of work to do, and as I contemplate this I pray daily for answers. I am grateful that I get to walk with others who seek a better way to live, one that is more inclusive and that follows the teachings embedded in "all my relations."

There have been so many full-circle moments in my life. One that stands out began in 1985, when in early sobriety my sponsor invited me to view the movie *The Honour of All: The Story of Alkali Lake*. I saw my own family in that movie. It had people who looked like my Métis relatives. Seeing the drinking and the violence, the way it affected young children, cracked me open and made me all the more committed to sobriety. It gave me hope, and I never imagined that one day I would not only be a writer but also that I would be hosting a reading for Word Vancouver that featured *Resolve: The Story of the Chelsea Family and a First Nation Community's Will to Heal*, a book about the Esk'etemc (Alkali Lake) People's journey with recovery. I give thanks for all who have walked before me, for those who so bravely shared their stories allowing me to release my shame, one little piece at a time.

BREAKING NEWS

there are many untold
stories unfolding in silence
there was no breaking news
when Maria Campbell
took us Métis storytellers to a hill
where a cross
visible from afar
marked the land   the rock where
prayer ties have been laid
since Time Immemorial
the rock now painted
blue for the Virgin
her outstretched arms and the cross
laying claim to the land and the rock
where prayer ties have been laid
since Time Immemorial

no one acknowledges

         this breaking

WHITE FLAG

my body is a war
nobody is winning.

—LUCILLE CLIFTON

"the message of jo," *The Collected Poems*
of Lucille Clifton, 1965–2010 (2012)

for some time now I have been
at war with this body

we were once friends
climbing trees together
our senses alive
the smell of the forest
filling our nostrils with hope

later when older the scent of a man
would drift towards us   we would be
on the edge of explosion – multi-orgasmic

we radiated outward with ease
but now – the bones in my feet tap tap tap
sending pain vibrations throughout

my exterior has grown larger with age
my once-small body is now her own planet
with many Moon-children circling   circling
unaware it is their care that sent me
into this downward spiral
falling inward   I no longer seek pleasure

what I seek now is peace
having surrendered I wave that white flag
there is no winning   that was a lie

AND WHAT ELSE?

for ingrid rose

> *Shame is corrosive to empathy.*
> —BRENÉ BROWN

skin glides over bone
protecting my heart
I offer my body OM sounds

my feet on the ground
sky connected
surrounded by air
ingrid drops words into my body
some sink   become shipwrecks
until I breathing the earth
can feel the spaces between
ingrid's words travelling inward
she asks *and what else?*

what else does my body have to say
I don't always like what it is telling me

the layers of loss hold muscles tight
cells colliding, dividing until I am made new

and what else?

becomes my mantra
there is always so much to let go of

TO BE A WOMAN IS TO BE MAGIC

I have been woman
for a long time
beware my smile
I am treacherous with old magic

—AUDRE LORDE

"A Woman Speaks," *The Collected*
Poems of Audre Lorde (2000)

I wanted to be Santana's Black Magic Woman
to feel his guitar fingers thrumming through
my whole body telling me
he sees women like me
he knows we are filled with magic
that a little colour makes us
more powerful   not less
I can still hear his call for us
to be that *black magic woman*

long ago he put a spell on me
I would have followed him anywhere
fifty years later I stand next to my son
on the floor of the arena when I hear
his siren song   I am still his
I can feel his guitar fingers

thrumming through my whole body

now that I am old

          can he still see me?

ALL MY RELATIONS

my body a universe
filled with glial-cell galaxies
shooting light
bringing healing
to limbs outstretched

within my reach a star
at my centre a galaxy
in my skin kin worlds
painful memories swirling
next to an ocean of joy

my brothers who shared the same space
within the universe of my mother's body
are gone but still with me
she is gone but still with me
all the Ancestors are gone but still with me

my body a universe
whispers blood-quantum stories
tells of time passing
transcriptional streaks of light travelling

        from cell to cell

an oscillating rhythm   holds my place

        calls out to the land

my body a universe
sits waiting for me to attend to it
within my reach a star
at my centre a galaxy
in my skin kin worlds
painful memories swirling
next to an ocean of joy

Forgiveness:
It's Never Too Late

Each human is a complex, contradictory story.

—JOY HARJO

"Each human is a complex, contradictory story...,"
Conflict Resolution for Holy Beings (2015)

My father visited me yesterday. I had just finished praying and leaving some tobacco in Queen's Park, a place I visit most days. I have thought of him often since reading *Rooster Town* and beginning to more fully appreciate the hostility he faced as a Métis. I have known about the disdain so many, including some of my white family, had for Indigenous Peoples. I have felt it since I was six years old. As a young child I was a witness to my father's pain. I was a sponge sucking in his fear, his rage, and all of his unshed tears. I remember the day his mother, my grandma Rose, told me that when my dad was a child, "he was a big baby," and that "he cried all the time." This said with the same disdain I had heard so often in my father's voice when he was upset with me for crying. As a mother I found her words unsettling, especially since my father had lost his father when he was just two and a half. As I contemplated this and the graves of the 215 little ones at the site of the former Kamloops Indian Residential School, I thought of the tears they must have shed. I don't know if anyone in my family attended a residential school, but I do know that my grandma Rose went to a Catholic day school where she was probably taught not to cry. Like so many other Indigenous people, I have lived in the echo of the spiteful words and actions of nuns and priests.

All of my adult life, I longed for some kind of resolution with my father, and when he died a few years ago I had to let go of that dream. We were so alike. It is he that I most related to. A handsome man, he was accomplished both at work and in sports like hockey, where he was known for his skill as a goalie. Not one to brag, he never told us that he had been offered a contract with the Montréal Canadiens' farm team and a tryout with the Habs. He turned it down, as he would not have been able to earn enough to take care of us and to buy that home. I see now all that he sacrificed and that his anger with me was not about me. I see now that he and my mother had a deep love for one another and that I was wrong to question her on this. She did not stay because she was weak. She stayed because she did love him and felt it was the best thing for all of us if we stayed together. I think of all my Indigenous friends, ex-boyfriends who were taken from their families, either so that they could attend residential school or as part of the Sixties Scoop. I give thanks all the time that I was not taken. Despite the violence in my home, I belonged with my parents. I know this may surprise some people, but I have heard enough from those who were taken to know that at least I felt loved, was able to stay with my brothers and be a part of my large extended families on both sides. I would advocate for families staying together, and if they are having the kind of trouble mine were, that they be offered support. I give thanks that I was able to break the chain of alcoholism and domestic violence. I could not have done this alone. So many walked with me, including my mother, who over the years has provided much-needed assistance from the other side. Now I have my father as well. When he came to me on that bench, he was a young man, the way I remember him when I was a small child. He was his soft self, the one who welcomed me into this world. The one who made me feel loved, who could see me. His pain took him away from me, but now he has returned to me.

It has been a long journey since that day in the oncologist's office where he told me my mother was dying. Without her I careened through life, at times reckless. I was lost without her. I became self-destructive. Adding to this, like my father, I did not fit in this colonized world. It is not my way.

I am a weaving of two cultures. An Icelander and a Métis. I am as the Creator intended. There really is no more to say. I have said enough and will leave you with some words from my grandmother, Jónína Gudrun Buason, wife of Cecil Denham, the mother of seventeen children, one of them my mother, Lorraine:

Love and respect our Land, water, and air. Respect the animals, birds, insects, fish, and their habitat. This will help our world to stay beautiful and healthy.

ROOTED

for my niece Gabby

I am rooted, but I flow.

—VIRGINIA WOOLF
The Waves (1931)

I am a story within the stories of many
I am a paradox
one thing and then another
parts of a whole
that does not know itself

turning towards the invisible
I can see the limits of knowledge
the places where formulas dissolve
into knowing that can only come
when quiet and walking in a forest
where the standing ones watch and wait
for us to return to ourselves
to the new stories that are waiting to unfold

ALL IS WELL

my body houses thought patterns
deep ridges etched on bone
where feelings roam like rivers
searching for an outlet
until I learn to breathe underwater
and within silence find an ocean
where all is well

it is always there
unchanged by grief   by worry
it remains silent waiting
for me to remember
my body can be a place of peace
where I am held
by gentle salt water
where I can swim in the ocean
that waits for me to dip my toes
and then my legs until
I am fully immersed in silence
where all is well

TUMBLING

there are rocks in my pocket   one for each death

the first rocks my Ancestors whispering thin
easily airborne skipping over waters of the past
these brought comfort   became touchstones
but then came the drowning   my brother sixteen
now a river rock made smooth by loss
sits next to the others
four years later a bullet   my brother eighteen
his rock marked by mushrooming metal

                        leaving a hole in him   in me

before long another rock
this one larger as it was mother
aunties   uncles   grandmothers
grandfathers followed

for so long I carried the dead
afraid to let them go I brought them everywhere
others could not see the rocks in my pockets
they could not hear the tumbling
did not feel the heat from the rubbing
against one another

every rock heavier than the last   harder to carry
yet together we all walked   losses rubbing up against one another
pressing on my thighs
until falling open seams stretched
emptying my pockets

I have been carrying the dead my whole life

                        I had to let them go

WHAT ENDURES

writers often wonder
will our words live on
once our time is passed
perhaps our wills should say

burn my books   especially the journals

all thoughts made public   delete them too
let us fade into the foreverness
no one need know we were here

perhaps it is time for others
to bring us better words for these times
let them fill the page with the new
unless we are like Rumi – timeless

some of us have been here before
and we will return again

                even if only through our words

WITHIN THE ECHOES OF ERASURE

When you realize reality is forgetting itself, forgetting you.

           Erased before you began. You try to hold on.

      But no one cares for your stories.

Your father's words, a virus entering cells, infiltrating thought
patterns.

           Until one day you see yourself in the mirror.

    You are old now. You have missed so

      much living erased.

Vaccinations arrive in the form of books meant to inoculate you

         from the stories that are not yours.

There are others like you. You are not alone.

     You will not be forgotten.

You are old now. You have something

       you want to say.

Your words on pages form new thought patterns.

        Some more true than others.

You are old now. There is no one here

      to correct you.

       You can create new pathways, tell new stories.

Rewriting reality your best defence.

NOTES

Although I was born in my Métis homeland, I have been an uninvited guest in many parts of what we now call Canada. Given this, there are a number of Land acknowledgments throughout this book. I used native-land.ca to locate a number of the Traditional and Ancestral Indigenous Territorial names. I also called on the kind assistance of Talonbooks editor Charles Simard. It is important to remember that precontact throughout Turtle Island, there were no borders between the US, Canada, and Mexico and that the Land was often shared by many Nations. The concepts of borders and land ownership are colonial constructs that have caused a lot of damage to all Indigenous communities on Turtle Island.

DISPLACED: IT'S ALWAYS ABOUT THE LAND
In the prose: **It was inconvenient, but … had become a symbol to Winnipeggers** is from Ariel Gordon, *Treed: Walking in Canada's Urban Forests* (2019), 79. Were it not for Ariel's work on this book, I would not have known that it was my great-great-aunt Mary Ann (Kirton) Good who planted the famous Wolsey tree or that she did this with the assistance of my great-great-grandfather Peter Kirton. Although this is rarely mentioned, I do believe they were Métis. Whatever the case, Peter Kirton married the daughter of my great-great-grandfather Waccan Jean Baptiste Boucher, a Métis interpreter and guide who brought Simon Fraser to New Caledonia, which we now call British Columbia. Waccan married my great-great-great-grandmother Nancy McDougall, the daughter of a Tse'khene woman (whose name is unrecorded) and James McDougall, Simon Fraser's third in command. Both James McDougall and Waccan settled in Fort St. James, BC, where they worked for the Hudson's Bay Company. My feelings of pride in this ancestral connection are mixed with deep concern for the fact that they would no doubt have assisted in the colonizing of those Lands. I often wonder if they knew what they were bringing to the people they both loved. History books rarely mention Waccan, and when they do, it is generally Métis historians who say he was a fearless man, well loved and respected by the local Indigenous people. Given the way history has been recorded by the "winners," I am not sure whether or not I can trust these accounts. One thing I am certain about is that

his descendants, who are in my lineage, have all been hard workers, community members who are strong and fearless. I see this in my own son.

The Passage was frequently used by Métis buffalo hunters … is from Lawrence J. Barkwell, "Metis Residents of Charleswood (St. Charles Parish)." I am so very grateful to Lawrence J. Barkwell, Scribd, and the Louis Riel Institute for the research and documenting of not only Métis history but also of the stories shared about my own Métis Ancestors. Without their tireless work, I would not know who I came from, and learning more about those whose steps I follow in has given me courage and pride. Understanding my Ancestors' roles in community, resistance, and things like the buffalo hunts has helped me to understand my own nature. Being able to pass on this knowledge to the next generation brings me great joy, as being without it for half of my life did contribute to my feelings of being lost and uncertain about my place in the world.

In "untethered," **Turtle Mountain**: My great-great-great-grandfather Osh-pih-kah-kahn Louis Godin III was one of the Métis who signed a petition for the Turtle Mountain Band Land Claim of 1891. The Turtle Mountain Band in North Dakota has a rich Métis history. If you would like to know more, see North Dakota Department of Public Instruction, *The History and Culture of the Turtle Mountain Band of Chippewa* (1997), www.ndsu.edu/fileadmin/centers/americanindian -health/files/History_and_Culture_Turtle_Mountain.pdf.

BELONGING: BREAKING THE CURSE
In the prose: **I once heard Fred Wah say it on a podcast when describing life as one who was biracial.** Sadly, the podcast is no longer available. Fred Wah has confirmed that he has used "standing in the doorway" when speaking about how it felt to be biracial.

In "erasure," **the result of the love of thousands** is from Linda Hogan, *Dwellings: A Spiritual History of the Living World* (1996).

The census data following "erasure" was found at Scribd.com. Permission to reprint was requested from the Louis Riel Institute, but no reply was received at time of publication. Talonbooks asks anyone with information relating to rights for this material to contact them.

BLENDED: A FAMILY CONSTRUCTED, THEN DECONSTRUCTED

In "the bereaved," **mirage of tenderness** is from Simone de Beauvoir, *The Second Sex* (1949).

BESIDE A WELL: WALKING WITH WOMEN

In the prose: the **Nüshu text** was found in Terry Tempest Williams, *When Women Were Birds: Fifty-Four Variations on Voice* (2012).

MOVEMENT: BODIES AND BOUNDARIES

In the prose: **My uncle Clarence Campeau.** Growing up, I had many blond, blue-eyed aunties, uncles, and cousins on my mother's side. At family gatherings, I always felt that I stuck out. Our family photos could have had the caption "One of these is not like the others." When I was a teenager, my mother's younger sister, my aunt Elaine, married Clarence Campeau, a Métis man who was very political. Clarence was always kind to me and for years he encouraged me to get what we called "Métis status" in those days. I have fond memories of him coming to Vancouver for a Métis national meeting. I recall one night sitting with him and other Métis who were active in our community as they all discussed what we needed. I was not yet ready to apply for my status, but I did often engage in debate with my uncle. He would say we needed education, jobs, self-employment, and I would say we needed to heal first. Over thirty years later, I now see that we were both right. Without a decent standard of living, all the healing is undone by the many demeaning moments that come with poverty. This I can attest to through personal experience. On the other side, I have seen those who do move up financially but don't attend to healing simply become colonized victims spreading the gospel of consumerism, the very thing that almost robbed us of our core beliefs. Despite all these things, we were and still are Otipemisiwak – the people who own themselves. Resistance is in our blood.

I am so grateful to my uncle, to all who have worked so tirelessly to bring us together, to maintain our traditions and teachings, and to assist those coming behind them to have more opportunities for education and health care, etc. It was the Métis Nation of BC that paid my tuition at the Simon Fraser University's Writer's Studio, where I graduated in 2007. Without their assistance I may never have become a writer and certainly would not be the writer I am today. Sadly, my uncle Clarence passed away before I could properly thank him. I remain very close to his wife, my auntie, Elaine Denham, who worked by his side. She is my favourite auntie and the one who most reminds me of my dear mother.

For more information, see "Clarence Campeau: Métis visionary leader, promoted education success," Windspeaker.com, December 9, 2017, windspeaker.com/news/footprints/clarence -campeau-metis-visionary-leader-promoted-education-success, and "Who Is Clarence Campeau?," *Northern Pride*, November 1, 2019, northernprideml.com/2019/11/who-is-clarence-campeau/.

WORKS CITED

Barkwell, Lawrence J. "Godon, Louis III (b. 1836)." Sribd.com. Accessed October 13, 2021. www.scribd.com/document/407722573/Godon-Louis-III-b-1836.

―――. "Metis Residents of Charleswood (St. Charles Parish)." Sribd.com, July 2018. Accessed October 13, 2021. www.scribd.com/document/383334056/Metis-Residents-of-Charleswood.

Beauvoir, Simone de. *The Second Sex*. Translated by Constance Borde and Sheila Malovany-Chevallier. New York: Alfred A. Knopf, 2010. French edition first published 1949.

Gilbert, Elizabeth. *Eat, Pray, Love: One Woman's Search for Everything across Italy, India and Indonesia*. New York: Penguin, 2006.

Gordon, Ariel. *Treed: Walking in Canada's Urban Forests*. Hamilton, ON: Wolsak & Wynn, 2019.

Hogan, Linda. *Dwellings: A Spiritual History of the Living World*. New York: Simon & Schuster, 1996.

Lucas, Phil, dir. *The Honour of All: The Story of Alkali Lake*. Vancouver, BC: Phil Lucas Productions, 1986. vimeo.com/ondemand/honourofall.

Parks Mintz, Carolyn, with Andy Chelsea and Phyllis Chelsea. *Resolve: The Story of the Chelsea Family and a First Nation Community's Will to Heal*. Halfmoon Bay [xwilkway], BC: Caitlin Press, 2019.

Peters, Evelyn J., Matthew Stock, and Adrian Werner. *Rooster Town: The History of an Urban Métis Community, 1901–1961*. Winnipeg: University of Manitoba Press, 2018.

Somé, Malidoma Patrice. *Ritual: Power, Healing and Community*. New York: Penguin, 1997.

Williams, Terry Tempest. *When Women Were Birds: Fifty-Four Variations on Voice*. New York: Sarah Crichton Books, 2012.

Woititz, Janet Geringer. *The Struggle for Intimacy*. Deerfield Beach, FL: Health Communications, 1990.

ACKNOWLEDGMENTS

I give thanks to every writer I have sat in circle with who has offered their teachings, their feedback, as I made my way with words. As a late-blooming poet, I had so much to learn, and in more recent years it has felt good to give back, to support writers who like myself have lived on the edge of things and had stories to tell.

The Canlit world is vibrant and at times messy. There are inner and outer circles and all the usual dynamics one would find in a dysfunctional family. It was often the younger writers who reminded me to dream and who have shown me that I had grown accustomed to things I had once resisted and fought against. Their courage and leadership allowed me to see that I had been worn down and made numb. Over and over again, other writers and activists gave me the language and the teachings I needed to regain my strength, to find my voice … that of an older woman who speaks and acts more slowly than she once did. I live with a chronic health condition and am limited in what I can do. I hold my hands up to all who are showing us the way towards a more inclusive literary.

I feel blessed to have a publisher like Talonbooks. Catriona Strang was the editor for this collection. Her capacity to keep track of all that a book like this needs to include was at times humbling. She was more than just a copy editor. She was always there to offer encouragement and support when I fell into the black hole of trauma, her feedback offered with care. I am very grateful to her.

I asked Jan Castillo to do the cover art. I met him when he was a part of the Wall-to-Wall Mural & Culture Festival in Winnipeg and was the artist chosen to create a wall mural using an excerpt from my poem, "untethered." I was so grateful for the time he took to understand the poem so that he could create what I can now see was a precursor to this book. In the mural my hair is a river with my words floating on the surface. It can be seen at www.walltowallwpg.com/untethered. He has once again outdone himself with this book cover image. The first time I saw it I recognized this woman. She is me. She is my grandmother. She is all Indigenous women.

Joanne Arnott, another Indigenous/settler, with ties to my birth-place, Portage la Prairie, was my substantive editor. She has been my Poet Elder since I first went to see her talk about Métis Diaspora in 2007. Her feedback brought ruptures that opened the book into areas I had not originally planned to go. With her kind assistance, I was able to go deeper into some trauma and then, with her encouragement, I also explored some happier memories. A mother of six, she is a fierce momma bear. A good woman to have on your side, to have your back.

It was Betsy Warland who opened my eyes to the possibilities that lie in cross-genre writing. Some stories want to be poems. Some ask to be more fully fleshed out. Being able to move between poetry and prose made it possible for me to follow my inner guidance.

There are so many to thank. Some I turned to when fear gripped my heart and I wanted to run away from what I knew I needed to tell. Chelene Knight was one of my strongest supporters. From our days on the *Room* editorial board to now, she has been a steadying presence in my life. She has a way of making you feel you can do it… whatever "it" is. She is one who always reminds me that she has my back. Whenever she says this, I feel my whole body relax. I trust her.

It is my husband, Garry Ward, who deserves the deepest of thanks. Living with a writer is not easy, especially when space and finances are limited. He has been my biggest supporter from day one, when I told him I wanted to apply to the Simon Fraser University's Writer's Studio. He is a poet himself and is always my first reader.

Some of these poems have appeared in earlier versions in the following publications: *Contemporary Verse 2* (CV2), *Room Magazine*, "ndncountry" (a special joint issue of *Prairie Fire* and CV2), *A Journey across New Westminster by Word: A Poetry of Place*, and *Another Dysfunctional Cancer Poem Anthology*. Thanks to their editors.

I give thanks to all funding agencies that make it possible for us to write and publish. I give a special thanks to the Canada Council and the BC Arts Council for their assistance with this book.

All my Relations
Jónína Kirton

Jónína Kirton, a Red River Métis/Icelandic poet, graduated from the Simon Fraser University Writer's Studio in 2007, where she is now an instructor. Although she acknowledges and is thankful for the teachings offered through academic institutions, she leans heavily into what some term "other ways of knowing." Her writing is often a weaving of body and land, as she firmly believes that until we care for women's bodies we will not care for the earth.

A late-blooming poet, she was sixty-one when she received the City of Vancouver's 2016 Mayor's Arts Award for an Emerging Artist in the Literary Arts category. Her second collection of poetry, *An Honest Woman*, was a finalist for the 2018 Dorothy Livesay Poetry Prize.

A landless Métis citizen, she currently lives in New Westminster, British Columbia, the unceded territory of many Coast Salish Nations, including the Qayqayt, Stó:lō, sc̓əwaθən məsteyəxʷ (Tsawwassen), xʷməθkʷəy̓əm (Musqueam), Sḵwx̱wú7mesh (Squamish), səl̓ilwətaʔɬ (Tsleil-Waututh), kʷikʷəƛ̓əm (Kwikwetlem), Stz'uminus, q̓icə̓y̓ (Katzie), and q̓ʷa:n̓ƛ̓ən̓ (Kwantlen).